For my husband, Keith.
Who will forever be my greatest blessing.

SONG OF SOLOMON 3:4
For I have found the one whom
my soul loves.

"Carrie's book is indeed the Trinity. In many ways it is autobiographical but not her entire life story; in some ways it is religious, but not in a pushy way; in other ways it is full of Southern charm and wit, but not so much that an outsider couldn't understand it. *From the Grit Comes a Pearl* is a hilarious look at life that most readers can relate to, especially females, as Carrie drives you down her own life journey. The stops along the way are filled with metaphors and similes that cause you to laugh and perhaps even shed a tear here and there. Highly recommend it."

—Mark Elley, author of John Doyle Mysteries

"I love Carrie's book and I love her Southern way of approaching things and telling it like it is with no second-guessing her. *From the Grit Comes a Pearl* is very easy to read and has many truths from the Scriptures and life lessons mixed within. Her book honors God, and you know where she stands with Him! Great job, Carrie! I highly recommend it!"

—Randy Plummer, author of Snowdeer Christmas Story, and musician, The Plummer Family Country Music Show

"I think my Southern drawl just got a little stronger! It didn't even feel like I was reading—I felt like Carrie and I were sitting on her back porch with a glass of wine laughing until we cried at stories of her life. I'm recommending her book, *From the Grit Comes a Pearl,* to all my friends who need a little encouragement and laughter from true experiences."

—Tennille Michel, a fellow strong, sassy Southern woman, devoted wife, and mom to four sweet boys, Kirbyville, Missouri

From the Grit Comes a Pearl

by Carrie Scarborough Kinnard

ISBN 978-1-64663-199-5

Published by

 köehlerbooks™

3705 Shore Drive
Virginia Beach, VA 23455
800-435-4811
www.koehlerbooks.com

FROM THE GRIT COMES A PEARL

*A Southern Woman's Imperfect Faith in Her God,
in Herself, and in Her Humorous, Unique Outlook
on Life's Stumbling Blocks*

CARRIE SCARBOROUGH KINNARD

VIRGINIA BEACH
CAPE CHARLES

CHAPTER 1

IF ON THAT FIRST DATE,
TOILET PAPER CROSSES YOUR MIND
. . . HE AIN'T THE ONE.

You see, he was cute.

Quite possibly the cutest boy in the world.

Okay, well . . . he was cute in his pictures. The two pictures he posted online. Two. Only two. But he was cute.

Online. A word that makes me cringe. But it's how we met.

Was this really a chance I wanted to take? And at my age?

At forty-three years old, I really felt I was too old to do anything online, much less, uh . . . date.

And I never wanted to say, "Meet my husband. We met online."

Years later, I still cringe at saying the words, "We met online."

I mean, in those last nine years of being single, I'd always felt the best part of a relationship was probably the very beginning. You know, when you hadn't met yet and you're still single.

You heard me. When you hadn't met yet and you're still single.

I'll admit, I also never wanted to say, "Oh, we met at a bar." Or at a wedding. Or the produce aisle. Or, Heaven forbid, church. Because that's too hip. Too young. Too not me. And I don't know why because everybody's doing it. But if everybody was jumping off a cliff, I can assure you, I wouldn't be surveying just how far the drop was.

Or, apparently, it seems now? I would be.

Meeting a man for the first time in person who you *met* online feels a lot like *Let's Make a Deal*. The old version. Monty Hall's version. Monty tells you to pick door one, door two, or door three. Then you close your eyes. Scrunch your face up a bit. Kinda maybe hold your breath a little. Clinch your fists in front of you. Squint a peek through one scrunched-up kinda closed eye. Hope to God the deal behind the door you pick . . . is at the very least . . . cute. Say a quick prayer before the curtain rises. Pray he has teeth. And a job. And no wife. And he looks somewhat like the pictures he sent you. A little like the pictures. Kinda like the pictures. Okay, just pray he has a head.

Anyway, in our first emails, we traded pleasantries. Typical stupid stuff. How long we each lived in the area. What we did for a living. Whether we had friends and how many. Any kids bleeding us dry? Boring. Blah. But necessary.

The second emails were just as nice. Easy. No inappropriate questions. No mention of the word boobs. Or sex.

But a very unexpected bomb was dropped. And that bomb was dropped on the very last few lines of his second email to me. This was a man I had not spoken to on the phone. A man I had only traded one, working on a second, email with. A man who I knew very little about. And this was how he decides to end his second email to me?

"Well, I am going to go out on a limb here and ask if your schedule would allow you to accompany me to dinner or drinks this weekend. You don't have to call it a date. Just two adults meeting to have dinner or drinks together. I am open Friday or Saturday evening. My daughter will be spending the weekend with friends, so I am seizing the opportunity to be Keith and not just Dad. I will keep my fingers crossed and hope I haven't scared you off."

BOOM.

What the what? A date? *Are you kidding me, dude?* We'd traded a few words electronically and you're pretty much proposing! Whatever happened to boring phone calls about nothing? All the *"Who cares?"* I needed to utter to myself while you're bragging about whatever it was you're telling me that I wasn't listening to? Where was all the waiting and wondering I was supposed to do? Where's all the *"please don't be him, please don't be him"* then *"crap, it's him"* when the phone showed his incoming number? Huh? Where was the norm here?

And okay, between you and me, I kinda liked it. I liked that he didn't go by the dude manual. Or playbook. Or whatever book it is that everybody else thinks exists but doesn't, yet they still try to follow it even while they're miserably failing. I secretly liked that he didn't play by the rules. Because Heaven knows, I sure don't.

Somewhere I read the definition of insanity was doing the same thing over and over and expecting different results. And in the past, I had done the same thing over and over. Then over and over again. I had done the three hundred eighty-six phone calls from a guy where he yammered just to hear himself yammer. I had read the five hundred twenty-three emails that basically said a lot of nothing. Then for some *I'm bored and got nothing to do on a Saturday night* reason, I had decided he was probably maybe okay enough to meet in person. Then I went on one date. One. Just one. Why one? Because he said boobs. Or mentioned sex. Or dribbled queso down his chin. Without noticing. While I was noticing for the rest of the evening.

This, though? A date on just no phone calls and two emails? That, my friend, was clearly insanity.

But I thought about it, and well . . . what did I have to lose? We would be in a very public place. Plenty of sharp objects on the table, if needed. If he didn't show, nobody would know. Well, except for that best girlfriend who always made me check in with her after each date to make sure I was safe. She would know. But, if he were a complete arrogant idiot, I could just excuse myself and go to the ladies' room. For years.

So we traded phone numbers, and Saturday night it was.

Just two nights away.

Still, no small talk phone call and no chatty text. No confirmation call and no confirmation text. No nothing.

But because he hadn't yet given me any reason to assume he was a flake, I stayed with the plans and gave it a go on Saturday night. And prayed he hadn't forgotten.

As I drove up to this swanky restaurant that he suggested, wearing that cute little blouse I just could not resist and those fancy new heels, I found myself wanting to heave. In a very ladylike and dainty way, of course. I was getting horribly nervous. And I don't get nervous. I actually couldn't remember the last time I got nervous. About anything, much less meeting some guy. Especially some guy I honestly didn't know truly existed. He was just a face on a computer monitor at this point. An email at the most. Just going to be another first date that I prayed wouldn't call again. Yeah, that's it. So why the nerves? Why the boob sweat? I mean, this here wasn't my first rodeo.

And I just mentioned boobs. Great.

It was just as I pulled up to the valet parking attendant that my phone dinged. And there it was: the text.

I was fully prepared to find out he was either going to be late or he was lost or his car wouldn't start. Or he already hated me and was texting to tell me he would not be calling after the date he wasn't showing up for.

Now, I decided to valet park to lessen the chances of stumbling in the parking lot in that fabulous pair of heels I just recently purchased and walking in to meet this man with a skinned knee and a tooth out. I had to forfeit the electricity bill in lieu of these heels, you know? Living sans lights was totally underrated when you had fabulous heels.

"Hi, Carrie . . . this is Keith. Tell the hostess your nervous date is waiting for you at our table."

I wanted to die. Right then and there, I wanted to see Jesus. I could already hear the angels humming "Amazing Grace." So, like I always say, "Go big or go home." Bring on Jesus. I was ready. Why waste this cute little blouse and these fancy heels on some guy when I had

Jesus, right? I immediately knew I could not do this. I could handle mentions of boobs or sex, but to have an *our* table was completely sending me upward and onward.

I stepped out of my car as the sweaty young man working the valet parking opened my door for me. Probably from the local college on his weekend job. It seemed he'd been jogging through this parking lot quite a bit by his heavy breathing. Or I'd like to believe I was just as pretty as a peach. Yes, that was it! No, no, it wasn't. It didn't matter. He was way too young, anyway. I mean, if he didn't know Lynyrd Skynyrd or the Bee Gees, he was too young. He took my keys, handed me this little retrieval card for later, and drove off in my car.

There I was. Standing alone in front of this swanky restaurant and just on the other side of those doors was a man. Waiting for me. At *our* table.

I pulled open a big, heavy wooden door and nervously approached the hostess. I didn't even know what to say. Did I ask for the dude at *our* table? Did I give her my name? Did I show her my fabulous heels then just run and leave?

"Yes, I'm here to meet someone for dinner. He's already here with a table."

No way could I utter the words *our table*.

She blankly looked at me, looked down at her little schedule of whatever it was hostesses looked at, then back at me, then back down at her little whatever.

"I'm sorry. I don't have anyone waiting."

What the what?

I knew it. I knew this was going to happen. It was just like in the movies. But I hadn't even actually seen this happen in the movies. This crap only happened to me. There I was, decked out in my fancy heels, perfect little fake diamond earrings, delicately placed lip gloss, and I was at the wrong swanky restaurant.

It was then another hostess walked up. The two whispered cheek to cheek while I felt my throat closing and my sight dimming. Then, just as I was certain I was losing consciousness, the second hostess blurted out, "Oh, yes . . . I just sat him upstairs! Follow me, please!"

Thank you, Jesus.

I followed her. She made small talk. Told me I looked fabulous. My nerves secretly thanked her for that. And that she loved my heels. My credit card secretly thanked her for that.

She stepped to the doorway of the room where my nervous date was waiting at our table and said, "Here you go, enjoy," and made a slight hand motion into the room.

I looked, and there were two men in the room where soft piano music played. Both at their own table. With white linens. Beautiful centerpieces. Soft glowing candles. Both with their backs to the door. Both with their backs to me.

I scrambled a bit, doing my best to not lose my balance in these *a little too high and probably should've practiced a bit more in* heels, and turned toward the hostess with, I was sure, a severely panicked expression of fear.

"Wait. I've never met him. Which one is he?"

She smiled and said, "Oh, he's very nice. He's right there." Then, as she motioned toward him, he turned toward me. He smiled. He rose from the table as I walked toward him. *Heels don't fail me now.* I could feel myself blush, and that was something I hadn't done since fifth grade when the boy in my English class asked if I would *go with him.*

Remember that? "Will you go with me?"

"Sure, dude, where? To the lunchroom, because you can't drive, and I can't date? So just *where* are we going at eleven years old?" Sorry, I'm rambling here.

Anyway, he was so cute, so handsome, so well dressed. He was so "all of that," I couldn't look at him. All I could hear myself say to myself was, *"Sweet heavens of all things really cute and no obvious nose hair, you're gonna have to do something about this, because this ain't just some ol' first date you're gonna be praying later doesn't call."*

I was not prepared to like a man. Much less enjoy a man's

attention. Or, Heaven forbid . . . fall in love with a man. That was way too much. I was simply dating to shut everyone up. Make people think I was on the prowl. You know, the big city single girl. Living life the way it's supposed to be lived. Free and easy. I had no intention of ever getting serious or much less marrying again. No way. No how. I had been single for nine years, and single fit me just fine. Wasn't too snug . . . not too loose. It fit really good. I liked the color. The feel. The way it moved. Being single was me.

Until now.

It felt like a three-day hike, but I finally made it to our table. He was standing, facing me, and gave me a very friendly hug. Nothing gropey. Or touchy-feely. Or creepy. He smelled heavenly. He pulled out my chair for me and helped me in my seat. For some strange reason, this was easy. He was easy. Things just felt natural. Completely opposite of anything and everything I'd ever known to happen for me on a first date.

We did the introductions, and his smile was perfect.

Keith.

He was very confident but not arrogant. Very kind but not weak. A gentleman. That's it. He was very much a gentleman.

He immediately admitted he was nervous. Very nervous. Which I was elated to hear. Because so was I. Like, my heart was beating incredibly hard. In my throat. And my ears, I was sure, were engulfed in flames. I was sure he could see it. But, because he admitted he was a bit nervous, that helped me be not so nervous. Because he was. But I still couldn't look at him. He was, like, quite possibly, the cutest boy in the world. And I was sitting with him. At "our" table. And he was smiling at me. And I couldn't hear anything he was saying because I was yammering to myself in my head and I wouldn't shut up telling myself how cute he was. And how nice. And how kind. And how perfectly dressed. And how different.

The more he talked, the easier this dating thing got. I was finding I'd rather talk to him than eat. And those words had never, ever left my mouth. Not for a man, anyway. I just wanted to sit there, look at him, and talk. With him.

Within a couple of minutes of being seated and doing the small talk, our waiter arrived.

"Pardon me, your wine." And he proceeded to place a lovely glass of wine at my setting. I wasn't sure what to do. I hadn't ordered any wine. I hadn't even looked at the menu at this point, because how rude would that be? Taking a seat then immediately flipping open the menu? I couldn't even think of food right now, anyway. Zero appetite. Which was completely foreign to me. As I said, no man had ever superseded my appetite. That right there should have told me something. I probably wouldn't have believed whatever it was that something was trying to tell me, anyway.

I was slightly panicking in my mind but somehow holding my charm at the table. This waiter was completely throwing me off. This kind of foul shot wasn't supposed to happen so soon in the game. I then said, "I'm sorry . . . I haven't ordered wine."

I figured the poor waiter already had his tables mixed up. Bless his heart. And Keith must be so embarrassed! First date and a bumbling waiter. This could only mean I'd end up with someone else's medium-rare porterhouse. Or someone else's salad dressing. Or, on a more positive note, someone else's dessert.

Keith then put his hand on my arm and said, "I hope it's all right, but I took the liberty of ordering your wine."

Gulp. Whoa. Fuzzy vision.

He touched me. On the arm. I was blushing again. My ears were on fire, and my heart was, again, back in my throat.

That, my friend, closed the deal.

A man who had the confidence to order my wine before I arrived? Just stick the ol' fork in my tush because I was done.

Call me old fashioned. Call me a little too southern. Call me dainty. Call me whatever you want. I can assure you I have been called worse. But I do like a man who takes the lead. Now, I didn't say a man who takes the reins or takes control . . . I said one who takes the lead. Big difference. Leading is much different than controlling or dictating.

So far, this evening was priceless. Let me tell you, this girl has been on plenty of first dates. And maybe three second dates. But this was a first for first dates. Ninety seconds into this gig, I wasn't going through my mental checklist reminding myself to pick up toilet paper on the way home.

And really, let's be honest here: if on that first date toilet paper crosses your mind . . . he ain't the one.

I wasn't thinking about that ridiculous project at the office I was nowhere close to finishing. That was due on Monday, by the way. I wasn't concentrating on not being too twangy with my southernness. I wasn't even troubled on whether or not my lipstick was smeared across my two front pearly whites.

I was focused on this terribly handsome man who had chosen to give me his attention for the next few hours. He never looked away from me. His focus was on me and whatever drivel came rolling out of my mouth.

It seemed we talked about everything. The conversation was effortless. Like two old friends reuniting after many years apart. He asked if it was okay that he left his cell phone on the table. Odd. Whatever. But fine. He proceeded to tell me his daughter was out of town with family friends heading to a concert. He needed to be available should she call.

Oh, yeah. That's right. A daughter. I forgot from his infamous second email. Great. And I didn't mean great in a great way. This must mean there's a mother lurking around the ol' ex-wife corner.

I thought it was nice of him to ask, but really? Would I say no to him being available for his daughter should she call? Uh, no. I would not. Plus, how would that look? Eight minutes into the date and I start cracking the whip?

I asked how old his daughter was. Because let's face it: no matter how bad I wanted a daughter when I was younger and in a much better child-rearing mental state, I wasn't raising some kid. Not now. Not at this age. Mother Goose, I was not. This was a date. Not some birthing room. She better have been off training wheels and able to choose her own lovely shade of shiny lip gloss and packing for college far, far away if a second date was even thought of. Don't tell me I had ballet classes and tooth fairies in my future. 'Cause that was not happening. I was too old to start that. I wasn't carpooling kids, and I wasn't girl scouting. I might be three gallons of crazy in a two-gallon bucket, but I wasn't doing it.

"She's fourteen."

Yuck. That's an odd age. Maybe doable. Maybe not doable. Not a toddler, but not in college, either. We're talking acne, sarcasm, folded arms, and eye rolling at its finest. And periods. Code Red! Code Red! The red moon would be rising once a month and just . . . NO. I couldn't do this. Not a girl. Maybe a little dude with his sweaty hair, smelly little armpits, and my endless reminders to go take a shower. But not a girl. I didn't need any help with drama in my life. I had a masters in drama from the University of MeMyselfAndI. And I didn't need any continuing education in that area, thank you very much.

Apparently, he could see the ick factor rising. Maybe it was my folded arms and eye rolling?

Now that we'd made our way through all the niceties on this date, it was time to get to the nut cuttin.' I asked a few questions about his daughter, hoping the mention of her mother would arise. No such luck. So I asked a few more. But he still said nothing of weekend tradeoffs, holiday exchanges, and blended family vacations. It seemed he was going to make me ask. He was going to make me walk that long path on a short pier of questions to *"So, tell me about her mother."*

"So, tell me about her mother."

All of this was happening over the best steak salad I'd ever indulged in while trying to appear "not very hungry" because that's how you should show up to a first date that consisted of dinner. Not very hungry.

And so, you get a salad. With steak on it.

"She doesn't know her mother. I guess you could say there really isn't one."

What the what? How did you not know your mother? Come on. I couldn't hide or run from my mother even at my age. I didn't even live with her and yet she reminded me before this date to be home by midnight. Why? *Because nothing is open after midnight but legs and the emergency room.*

He tells me her mother left when she was eighteen months old. Her mother chose a life of drugs and alcohol instead. So they divorced, and he had raised their daughter himself. There were no birthday cards, no Christmas presents, no summer vacations, no phone calls from Mom. Her grades were excellent, and she played sports, easily made friends, and accepted the fact there was no one to leave a Mother's Day card for on the kitchen counter each May.

Okay, then. So that's how you don't know your mother. Good to know. Or not.

Hearing this, it kinda made me like him a little more. I just lied to you. It made me like him a lot more. He was responsible. And committed. Instead of tossing her off for someone else to raise, he stuck it out. And while he was telling me about the last fourteen years, I was yammering to myself again in my head.

It might not be so bad to sit through a girls' softball game.

Being jerked around in the car by a new driver might not be the end of the world.

I always did like shopping for prom dresses.

And makeup. This girl is gonna need the proper lessons on lip gloss application!

This date was not even halfway over, and in my mind, I'd already married this man. As much as I was loathing myself for admitting to me that he was the one, I couldn't stop enjoying his company. Heaven knew I was trying. My nine-year streak of singlehood was coming to a screeching halt. Right there, right then, in front of my very lovestruck eyes.

And with that second glass of merlot, I might add.

Never had I ever done this. I was completely off my game and not looking for every reason to ditch this guy and leave. I hadn't even thought of the ladies' room disappearing act. I wouldn't let myself look at the time for fear it's late. If I didn't look, I couldn't leave, right?

More questions came and went. I couldn't find anything repulsive about him, and not once had he uttered the words "boobs" or "sex." Not once. The conversations were easy, and I might even say fun. Until he turned the tables and now it's my turn to answer a few of his questions.

After a few easy inquiries about my family life and friends and job and such, he went for it.

"What is something very important to you that you look to find in common with a man?"

Whoa. Well, okay, then. He opened the door now. I could either walk through it and risk scaring him off or, well, I could walk through it and risk scaring him off. So that's just what I did. I brought up one of the two subjects we in the South are taught to never bring up in public.

Politics. And religion.

Therefore, I'll take "Religion" for $1,000, Alex.

"Well, it's very important to me that I have a man who has a strong faith. He will go, without being asked, and sit with me in church. Again, without being asked. And he will hold my hand. I don't have to beg him to go with me or barter with him about it. He just does it because it's what he does. It's who he is."

And on that note, I figured I should just wrap this little soiree up while the getting was good. That right there should have cooked this goose and we're done. *Nice meeting you. I had a great time. Somebody find me that valet guy. Adios.*

"Well, that's something very important to me, as well. My daughter and I attend services most every Sunday morning, so I don't think that is going to be a problem for us."

Did he just say for *us*? First *our* and now *us*?

Dear Lord, can there be just one thing wrong with this man? Am I asking you for too much here? You're making it quite difficult for me to hope he doesn't call. Can you give me just one thing to justify me going to the ladies' room only to break a freshly manicured fingernail climbing out the window for?

Before I knew it, we were splitting carrot cake and coffee. It was getting close to midnight, and well, remember what Mother said about legs and emergency rooms? It was probably best I nailed this coffin shut and gave him an out.

With my arm in his, we walked through the big, heavy wooden doors to the outside. The heavy breathing valet parking attendant from earlier was no longer heavily breathing. He was pooped and ready to finish his tour of duty. He was now just waiting on a few folks to finish up their evening, collect his tips, and call it a night. I handed him my retrieval ticket, and he slowly trotted through the parking lot to retrieve my car. I was silently praying in my head *Dear Lord, don't let this man try to kiss me. Dear Lord, don't let this man try to kiss me.* I've never been one for that first date slobber fest at the end of the evening. Plus, I'd just reapplied lip gloss and, well, just . . . no.

As I was feverishly yammering to keep any chance of that dreaded kiss from happening, I felt Keith's hand on my lower back, and with one slight move, he pulled me in and placed the most perfect kiss on my lips.

That was it.

The best first kiss ever.

The last first kiss ever.

He didn't even smudge my lip gloss.

Once I was able to see straight again and all those annoying flashing lights stopped, all I could do was smile. And blush. And blush a little more.

By this time, the valet attendant was pulling up with my car. Keith opened my door and helped me in.

"I really hope I can see you again."

Again, I could hear the angels humming. But this time it was "How Great Thou Art."

"I would love that. Thank you."

He smiled, closed my door, and I drove off.

Fully expecting to never hear from him again. Because he was just that cute. Just that confident. Just that kind. You see, the "cute" and "confident" ones are the "kind" to not surface again. They like to play the field. Sow their oats.

But it was nice while it lasted. The food was incredible. The conversation was priceless. The date was heavenly.

I then did what any other God-fearing southern woman would do. I called one of my best girlfriends.

I had to promise to call her on my way home so she would know I was safe. Or maybe she wanted to make sure *he* was safe.

Lisa started asking questions without even greeting my call with a sweet and unassuming hello. Thank you very much, caller ID.

"Is he nice?"

"Does he have a job?"

"Does he have all his teeth?"

"What did y'all talk about?"

"What's his last name?"

I answered all of her questions without interrupting. I told her just how perfect everything seemed and how this was the easiest date of my life. It just felt natural and was pretty effortless. Once my heart got out of my throat and my ears were no longer on fire, that was.

"Carrie Kinnard. Wow. Now that has a good ring to it. It just rolls off your tongue easy. I'd say this is the one. You're gonna marry this man, Carrie Kinnard."

I squealed like a third-grade girl and giggled while telling her to stop putting all my eggs in his basket. I was not marrying this man, for this was only one date. The first date. Albeit, the best date of my life, but it was just one. I wasn't even sure this wasn't the only date. He had plenty of time to not call.

Once I was home and my face was washed and those *a little too high and probably should've practiced a bit more in* heels were off my aching feet and my comfy PJs were on my tired body, I said a little prayer. I thanked God for such a great date. Such a great time. And for such a kind and handsome man. This was a perfect night and a sweet reminder that those good men I thought were only married or gay but never single still were out there. And possibly available. And maybe, just maybe, I wouldn't be single for the rest of my life. Maybe all those secret prayers of finding *the one* would be answered. Maybe all those single years of not settling for mediocre would pay off. Maybe without even looking, I'd find *the one*.

The next morning, before my eyes opened, I heard a ding!

A text.

"I had a great evening and look forward to seeing you again."

Or maybe *the one* would find me.

You see, at the time, though I didn't realize it then, I just had my very last first date.

I mean, don't tell anyone and don't rub it in my face later, but I actually prayed this one *would* call again.

And he did.

So for all of you ladies who swear the good ones are taken and there are no good men left in this world, I thought the very same thing.

But I was never more wrong.

And now you are never more wrong.

You see, the good ones aren't out looking for the next kill, the hottest cleavage, the tightest skirt, or the fun "life of the party" girl.

No, they're sitting back very quietly.

And they're watching.

Watching for morals. Watching for standards. Watching for manners. Watching for self-respect that enters the room before you do.

That good one will see things in you, even you don't see.

And he'll court you. And he'll seek you. And he'll treat you with the respect you've never really felt before.

And you'll never, ever wonder with him.

Meaning, you'll never wonder what he's doing. Who he's talking to. Where he's going. Where he's been.

For he will always treat you as a lady deserves to be treated.

And you'll enjoy being treated like a lady.

Not a chick. Or a babe. Or a hottie. Or the flavor of the month.

A lady.

So, don't give up.

Hope. Pray. Hope some more. Pray some more. Live a good life. One that you are proud of. Be strong and independent and wise. Take care of yourself. Take care of your health. Never stop learning. Buy those heels. Have your nails done. Try on that dress. Get the lip gloss. Laugh with your girlfriends and cry with your best friend.

Tend to your spirit.

And he will find you.

Let him court you. Let him seek you. Let him cherish you.

Then let him be the man that he is, for the lady that you are.

Because you so deserve that.

And so, does he.

ROMANS 8:25

But if we hope for what we do not see,
we wait for it with patience.

CHAPTER 2

IF YOU'RE LOOKING FOR CHIVALRY, I BET IT'S HANGING OUT WHERE ALL THE BEING LADYLIKE IS HIDING.

You know when you know that you just know? I was pretty sure I knew.

I was pretty sure I knew this man was the one. I wasn't yet sold on the fact that he was the one I was going to marry and live a life of commitment with, but I did know he was not going to be just another first date.

But that's just what he was: another date. And then another. And another. And so on.

That second date was just one week after that first date. He asked if we could have an old-fashioned date. One where he picked me up, took me to supper, then took me back home and walked me to my door. Not where we met up, had a bite to eat, then he went this way and I went that way. No. He asked for a true date.

Yeah, down here in the South, most of us call it "supper." I mean, Jesus and his disciples didn't have the Last Dinner, did they?

Anyway, I agreed to it. I mean, how could I not? Plus, I liked "old-fashioned" anything. A lot of us girls, especially those of us raised in the South, still believe, come hell or high water, manners were to be minded. And manners are quickly becoming old-fashioned these days. Or so it seems. Therefore, when we find a man with those manners, a perfectly tweezed eyebrow is raised and attention is paid. We believe in arriving on time, that you can tell a lot about a man simply from his handshake, and that ladies like to hug.

Heck, I've participated in a *menage a hug* in the shoe aisle simply over that perfect shade of ecru.

We still cherish that ever-so-perfect southern table setting. The knife blade will always have the cutting edge toward the plate, and the dessert spoon is brought with the dessert. But don't even get me lying about those ever-dreaded dinner and salad forks. I don't know why we eat with a dinner fork at supper, but we do. I'm not sure any of us really know which is which. Or if they even really matter. Because odds are if *we* don't know which is which, then neither does he.

Anyway. It was a bit strange for me to agree to him picking me up at my place because, you see, no one knew where I lived. I mean, sure . . . I had an address. But I never really invited anyone to my place. Except for my family and a couple of really close friends. I didn't see the need for a single girl, living alone in a big city, to have a constant parade of visitors at her place. Probably one of the smarter things I've done in life.

For some reason, after that five-hour first date, I found myself feeling this man was trustworthy. So a true old-fashioned date it was.

Plus, it didn't hurt he was in law enforcement. The Man, the Fuzz, the Five-O. Okay. Sheriff's deputy. The man was a sheriff's deputy. You and I both know I'm not nearly as hip as I try to sound.

He arrived, and I met him at the door. Once again, very handsome. Perfectly dressed. I started that ridiculous blushing mess again. I could feel my ears heating up and my heart back up in my throat. I was maybe, somewhat hoping he'd show up in a ball cap and dirty shorts. That would be my out. This would be that last date with this dude that I was kinda, in a way, hoping for. I was really beginning to wonder who was dressing this man. On both dates, he was wearing something I would have most likely chosen for him if he asked. Was

CARRIE SCARBOROUGH KINNARD 19

there anyone asking, "You're not wearing that shirt, are you?" and so he changed it just before leaving for our dates? Anyone suggesting that he not wear that ball cap? Was he doing all this handsomeness on his own?

After I got seatbelted up and all tucked in my side of his vehicle, we chatted like two old friends.

Whoa. Did you hear that? Had I just said, "*My* side of his vehicle?" Was I already laying claim to a side?

After the first few minutes of the ride, the nerves disappeared. Just nice small talk about our week and things that were happening in the city, on the job, with the families.

We arrived. It looked to be a very nice restaurant, and he politely helped me out of his rather large truck that should have come with an extension ladder. You know, those southern boys do like their trucks big. He was very charming and certainly didn't seem to mind assisting me to ground level. Once out of his truck, I slipped my arm in his, strictly for balancing purposes in my leopard print heels, and into this hip and stylish restaurant we walked.

The place was rather busy and, well, it *was* a Saturday night and it *was* a ritzy part of the city and I *was* thinking he probably never thought to make reservations.

"Reservations for two, please. Last name Kinnard."

Well, I declare. More old-fashioned-ness to my surprise. Though it was the second date, I still had very small hopes of finding something wrong with him. Something I could blame my *still not dating anyone worth dragging to Momma's for Sunday brunch* life on. But so far, nothing. I was at a loss.

The hostess showed us to our table, and we took our seats. Beautiful table setting with white linens and a candle and topped off with a lovely bouquet fresh flowers perfectly placed across the table from the two of us. Water glasses were brought, menus were placed, and he was awkwardly side-peering at me while trying to pretend he was looking at his menu.

I wasn't sure how to react. What was it? Lipstick on my teeth? A smidgen of that Reese's Cup I snuck before he picked me up smeared on my chin? A zit? *Oh God, please no . . . not a zit. Not tonight. I'm forty-three and should be well past zit age. Don't do this to me, don't do this to me, do not do this to me!*

"Those are for you. I hope you like them."

I had no idea what he was talking about. Those what? I shuffled my eyes around the place really stealthily like and quickly noticed our table was the only table with . . . you guessed it: a lovely bouquet of fresh flowers.

I looked at the flowers. I looked at him. Then back at the flowers. Then I really wanted to kiss him right then and right there. But manners. Those things that kept me from swigging straight from the wine bottle in public. Those manners kept me intact. This was the most romance I'd had since, well, since . . . since our last date.

"Oh, my goodness. Really? They're perfect. They're beautiful. Thank you. I have never, ever had such an amazing surprise like this, and I love them!"

I could have very easily squealed like a stuck pig at the feed bucket, but thank heavens for manners.

That lovely bouquet of fresh flowers? Deal sealers.

Opening doors. Flowers. Pulling out your chair. You know, that chivalry stuff we ask about all the time and swear is dead?

Well, I don't think it's dead, after all.

If you're looking for chivalry, I bet it's hanging out where all the *being ladylike* is hiding.

On the first date, he was cute and confident and kind. On this second date, I was seeing another side of him. Now, he was handsome and charming and romantic. All this goodness wrapped up in one man? I must have been living way too good.

The evening progressed with laughs and conversation. I asked more questions than should have been legal about his job in law enforcement.

"Have you shot anyone?"

"Is your gun in your sock?"

"Ever said, 'Go ahead, make my day,' while pointing your gun?"

You know, all the stuff that only happened in movies and in my overactive imagination. There were more things I wanted to ask, like, "Ever seen a real live hooker and did she look like Julia Roberts?" and, "Do you have a CB radio in your car?"

Thank heavens I didn't ask *that*. CB radios are only found in 1976. And apparently in my mind.

This perfect gentleman I was sitting with was gaining my trust and my favor with every smile he sent my way.

When the evening was over and he was pulling back into my driveway, I decided right then and right there, *Pucker up, big boy*.

He got out of his side of the truck, walked to my side to help me out, and as soon as the door opened, I turned toward him and placed the best kiss I had hidden away right on his kisser. By the look on his face, this was not what he was expecting. Nor was I, to be honest with you. It had to be done before I lost all nerve. It had to be done before I convinced myself otherwise. It just had to be done.

Once all the flashing lights and twinkling stars dimmed and he could think straight again, he confessed he didn't expect that. However, he was glad it was done because now he didn't have to figure a way to make it happen. Like I've said so many times in life, *Go big or go home*. No sense in piddlin' around with the small stuff, right? Just take the bull by the horns.

Or the deputy by the badge.

He proceeded to walk me to my front door, sneak in one more little kiss on the cheek, then I waved and once again smelled my lovely flowers as he walked back to his truck.

Only to see him again the following week.

After that date, I knew things were going to be different. Not too many more Saturday nights alone at the movies were in my future. Very few Sunday afternoons flipping the remote by myself were eyeballing me. No more wondering if this was as good as life was going to get.

So, this is why I can say I knew when I earlier asked, "You know when you know that you just know?" It all started coming together in my mind within a month or so of his attention. At my age, it was easy to know. None of that:

So what are you gonna be when you grow up?

Where do you plan on settling down in life?

Do you want kids and how many?

When you're younger, so many questions come into play to sum up a relationship beyond compare. But being a bit older and knowing who you are and where you've been, it's a bit easier. We both were established in life and just had to figure out a way to make our two lives mesh with as little discomfort as possible.

I've come to learn that knowing where you've been plays a big part in where you're going. I can certainly tell you, because I knew where I had been in life simplified any decision making on where I was not going again. I may not be sure of where I'm going, but I can darn sure tell you where I'm not going. When you know where you've been, you don't waste time looking through that small rearview mirror anymore. Instead, you keep a steady, watchful, and excited gaze on that big, giant front windshield that can really lead you anywhere.

After a little more time spent together, he invited me to his house for supper. (We call it "supper" because, again . . . ever read in the Bible about the Last Dinner? I didn't think so.) He would prepare a meal, and it'd be a little less formal than our past dates. Very easy and relaxed. Except for one thing: that other woman he lived with would be there. His daughter.

Gulp.

Well, now. This was starting to sound official. Was I ready to move from very comfortable and casual to not very comfortable and not very casual? This was going to be like a first date all over again. I just didn't think my nerves could handle that. I was too old for this.

Goodness gracious, this was just pushing that envelope a little too close to the edge now.

Whoa. Wait a minute here. Let's think about this for just a second. By going to his house, I should have been able to determine, within the first four seconds of entering his home, if it held the ol' ex-wife's touch. Decorative candles? Vases of flowers? Matching placemats and napkins? Tampons? This shined a whole new light on things. This should determine how much of a future me and Mr. Moving Right Along might have had here.

Therefore, God willing and the creek doesn't rise, to his house I was going. With all my feelers out. And my feelers would be freshly manicured and polished, of course.

I arrived and was promptly met outside as I pulled into the driveway. The driveway attached to this beautiful home with lovely landscaping, mind you. I was met by Keith. And her. The daughter. She was smiling, so that was a good sign. No eyes rolling. No folded arms. And no acne. He opened my door, I received a nice hug, and introductions were made.

Her name was Cayla.

Us southern girls not only like to receive gifts, but Lordy mercy, we like to give 'em, too. So, God love it, I came prepared. In anticipation of our first meeting, I made a small purchase. A dainty little gold necklace with a cross. I hugged her, told her how nice it was to finally meet her, and handed her the pretty little felt pouch. Once opened, she lit up and was a squealing little sweet pea hopping like a rabbit and asking her daddy to secure it around her neck.

Another one of the smarter things I've done in life.

We headed to the front door, and I was prepared. Prepared to see fluffed tulle draperies, accent pillows galore, and delightful ruffles. Lots and lots of ruffles. Precious, ladylike ruffles. You know the kind that make you a bit queasy. Just an overload of feminineness.

As the three of us were kinda tripping over each other making our way through the doorway, I was scared to look beyond the foyer.

But I had to. So I took a big, deep breath and followed them into the living room with eyes wide shut.

Then there it was. The teller of all truths. Over the fireplace mantel. I looked away. I couldn't focus on it. It's worse than I expected. I never once prepared to see a face other than his or hers looking back at me in this house. But it was. I was stunned he invited me in knowing I would see this.

A skull. Not an ex-wife skull. At least I didn't think. More of a dead animal skull kind of some sort. Just hanging there. Over the fireplace mantel. Looking at me. Kinda staring. Kinda not.

"What in tarnation is THAT?" was what did not part my lips, but you know I was screaming it in my head. With a curse word or four. Though I do have my deep southern roots, don't think for one minute my "redneck ways" don't surface more often than I care to admit. I mean, I do love me some Jesus, but this mouth of mine should be in church more often than in a bucket of Bluebell.

That skull eyeballing me without eyeballs over the mantel completely eliminated any notion of a woman's touch in this house. No farther did I have to look. No snooping through the kitchen drawer for seasonal doilies, because what manly man with the slightest bit of testosterone would even say the word "doily," much less have Mardi Gras–themed table runners? No meddling through the bathroom cabinets for delicate items for "lady parts central," because what manly man with the slightest bit of testosterone would have, well . . . those things?

Future-wise, this man was looking better and better. Now, if only he could cook.

Because his home held no frou-frou feminine decor, I certainly did not expect to see, or really even want to see at this point, a proper table setting. That's my area. Never before had I uttered the words in my head, *Jesus, let there be paper plates and let them be sturdy and good ones, mind you, but paper, nonetheless, and please no gravy boats.* The more bachelor pad-like his place could be, the better. He should just stick to areas of life he was good in: surprising me with flowers and ordering my wine.

There were no paper plates, but there was a delicious meal of I don't even remember what, but it was scrumptious, I can tell you. All three of our plates matched, as did the glassware. Meaning there were no mismatched Tupperware plastic tumblers.

Cayla was a rather pleasant hostess. She was actually a delight. Her conversation skills rivaled many of my adult-acting friends. She could actually stay on topic, in other words. Her manners were impeccable. No interrupting and no teenage lingo. Though rather early in the game, should this relationship thing continue, she might not be a bad addition to my life.

After supper, everyone helped clear the table and put away dishes. Then we sat. And we laughed. And we talked. And we, meaning me, answered some *first date with his teenage daughter* questions. Such as:

"So, uh, why are you going out with him? I mean, he's a dad and all. And he's not really that cool."

And yes, that question did consist of a scrunchy face and squinty eyes. Because like all dads, her dad was so not cool. To her.

"Well, he's really nice. I find him very interesting. And we have a good time together."

She didn't look to believe that answer too much. She continued on with another question about my not having children. I felt if she was bold enough to ask, I was going to be bold enough to be honest.

"You see, I did try to have children when I was married before, but the doctors discovered I can't have children, Cayla. It's just not in the cards for me. So Keith having a daughter was also a plus in my book as another good reason to be going out with him."

"So, basically, after meeting me, you like him even more?"

"Okay. Yes, that would be fair to say."

She then turned to her dad, gave him a sly, teenager smile as only a sly teenager can do, and loudly whispered, "I told you she'd like me. And I like her, Dad. You should never date anyone else again."

And with that, she hugged my neck, thanked me for her necklace, made her way to her room, and lightly closed her door. To never be seen or heard from again that evening. Which, for the time being, made her quite the perfect child.

Because this was a work night, we wrapped up the evening fairly soon after that. Keith walked me to my car, thanked me for a nice evening and for making the drive to their house. It was at that time, after that kiss and hug, I knew there were going to be no other dates. With any other men, that was. This was it. And I was pretty certain he knew it, as well. Again, when you're my age, you just know. Being a bit older and knowing who you are and where you've been, it's a bit easier to know when it's right.

Without really realizing it, we found ourselves seeing each other more often. Once a weekend dates started turning into two or three times a week. Some dates were nice traditional dates. Some dates were simply sitting in the audience while attending Cayla's choir concert with him. Other dates were a backyard cookout or a Saturday matinee movie. And I say Saturday matinee because I don't do movies at any other time. Too talky and too people-y. And too much bag crunching and popcorn noise. Which means too many body smells in a too confined area. It would be on dates like that my "redneck ways" would supremely outweigh my "southern charm," and nobody wants that.

While out at supper one night with Cayla, the subject of sports came up. I don't know why. That is certainly not something I'd ever claim to know anything about. Sports. Blah. I'm not one of those southern women who loves her Monday Night Football or World Series. I could care less. But before I knew it, a snow ski trip to New Mexico was being planned. Cayla got the okay to invite a friend, and I had to figure out if ski boots could be bedazzled in precisely two months. Then it hit me that this was turning into long term. No more of this supper and a movie stuff. Long. Term.

I had to nip it. And nip it quick. You know, before I got too much more involved with this man who I really liked and was starting to love and was wondering how I enjoyed life before him and seeing there's no way I could have half the life I have without him. Yeah, that man. The one I thought about all the time. The one who had treated me better than I'd ever been treated. The one who, well, the one who just was. Him.

In plain English with my ridiculously heavy twang applied, this meant I was gettin' col' feet. (Drop the "d" at the end of "cold" and the word "feet" has two syllables. Accent on the second syllable. You're welcome.)

Come to think of it, he mentioned "future" stuff all the time. And by future, I mean more than a week out. He made small talk about upcoming holidays, where he'd like to go on a summer vacation, stuff like that. Smooth. Real smooth. I never even saw it coming. Until a few days later when the ski lift tickets were needing to be purchased.

That's when he heard those three little words no man ever wishes to have shoved into his ears: *Dude, we gotta talk.*

Okay. That's four words. But I'm no good at math, and who's counting, anyway?

I shot straight to the point. No dilly-dallying around here. No mincing words and mixing meat. Okay, I don't know what that means either, but you get what I'm saying.

"Listen. I do like you and all. A lot. I really do. More than any other loser I've gone out with. And no, you're not a loser, but you know what I mean. I'm just not sure this ski trip thing is a good idea. I mean, what are we doing here? Without talking about it, it seems we have decided to not see anyone else. Or at least I'm not and I think you're not. Like we're exclusive or something. A couple. But let me tell you, I am not going to get involved with some man, fall for him *and* his kid, then be kicked to the curb for some perky set of new boobs that come strolling up out of the blue. I need to know where I stand with you and where this thing is going."

Annnnd I just said boobs again. Just great.

He stared one of those lost, blank stares at me. He was frozen. Dumbstruck. Dazed. And that was when I laid it all on the line. That's when I dropped the bomb. The words that put his talking into doing:

"I'm telling you right here and right now, I am not going to be anyone's fifty-year-old girlfriend."

Another blank stare. But this time with squinty eyes. Like I was crazy or something. Whatever. Not the first time I'd seen *that* look.

And I just knew what was coming out of that man's mouth next. I just knew. I could tell by the slightly confused glint in his eyes. He was gonna very plainly tell me to calm down. Which, on us southern girls, works about as good as trying to baptize a cat.

However, it was then, at that time, he proposed the very thing I did not expect him to ever propose. The words I never dreamed would leave his mouth. The question I seriously had not thought of, until then.

"So, do you think we should do two-day or three-day ski lift passes?"

And then he smiled.

Later, I was told that's when he knew. He just knew.

That ski trip was one of our best trips ever. Cayla and her friend took one ski lesson and never looked back. Youth. Amazing how things come so much easier when you're young. It was as if they skied right out of the womb with ski bibs on. Keith did quite well and conquered the bunny slope like a pro. Me? I perfected falling off the ski lift with grace. It wasn't too difficult to do . . . it seemed to come naturally. And it was on this ski trip I discovered wine around a ski lodge sparkling fire is just as heavenly as, well, wine around a ski lodge sparkling fire.

A short three months later, in early spring, Keith wanted to have both of our families over to his place for a Saturday backyard cookout around the pool. Apparently, to him, we were a couple now.

Now, mind you, I'm not a lover of crowds or big shindigs. Or what I affectionately refer to as a *No Way No How*. Oh, don't get me wrong. I do enjoy them. When they're over and everyone has left. However, the anticipation and the planning and the grocery shopping leading up to such an event can send me through the roof. Don't even mention the cleaning beforehand. Then the cleaning after-hand. I end up getting on my own last nerve before it even begins. Then again when it's over. But this was something Keith wanted to do, and as of late, I was doing things with a smile I'd normally not do. Like, shave my legs twice in one week. Not openly curse in the church parking lot. Things like that.

The day arrived, and so did the family. All of 'em. Mommas, daddies, sisters, brothers-in-law, nieces, nephews, dogs. The whole shebang. Weather was just perfect, so that helped keep everyone outside and not inside scuffing up those floors I glistened sweat while mopping. Everyone seemed to be having a grand old time. Even me. And before I even knew it, this little party was not far from coming to a grand ol' close. I was surviving.

Just as I found myself enjoying that second glass of wine and not thinking about the mound of dishes to be washed from all this so-called "fun," I heard Cayla giggling from somewhere off around the corner behind me. I paid no mind to it until I heard her say, "Hey, Carrie . . . look!" I could hear giggling and a bunch of rustling around back there with her. The kids in my family are usually up to no good. I was fully expecting to have a fake snake thrown at me. Or a fully loaded water gun discharged. Because come on . . . I'm related to these kids and I've taught them well.

I shifted around in my chair, and there they came. The pack of nieces and nephews. One right after the other. Each holding a big hand-painted sign. One by one, they each lined up and stood behind me, which was now in front of me because, in my frozen state of the fear of not knowing what they're up to, I'd shifted around in a very awkward position in my chair.

"*Will*" is written on the first sign.

"*You*" on the second.

"*Marry*" the third.

And Cayla was the last one in line holding the last sign that simply had the words, "*My Dad?*"

So there it was: *Will You Marry My Dad?* in big bright kid-script letters.

Of course, it took me a few seconds to actually realize who this was for and what it meant. Before I knew it, in what felt like slow motion, I belted out the words, "*Oh, my sweet Lord in Heaven above,*" my eyes twice the size of my face. I turned to get out of my chair, and there he was. In front of me. On bended knee. With a little ring box in his hand.

I could tell by the smiles, cheers, claps, hoots, and hollers coming from the rest of the family I was the only one not in on this little secret. For the first time, in quite possibly my entire life, I had no words. Not even any good ol' ladylike curse words.

I'm sure Keith said some really nice things at that moment. Probably stuff like how he'd never been happier. He couldn't imagine life without me. I was the only woman for him. He'd never seen a lovelier shade of lip gloss. But honestly, I don't remember a thing. Other than throwing my hands over my eyes and squealing. And trying not to cry. And hoping Mother wasn't snapping a camera if my lip gloss had worn off.

It was then I knew that I knew that I finally just knew. I knew Keith was the one who would forever make me blush, make my ears feel on fire and like my heart was in my throat. I knew he was the one I was going to marry and live a life of commitment with. I finally just knew.

It was two weeks later, on a Thursday, I left work early. I drove to what had become my new home. It was there on that Thursday afternoon that Keith and I stood in our living room, with Cayla and the pastor, and made our vows to each other.

No family, no friends. Just us. The beginning of our new life together.

You see, we didn't want a wedding. We wanted a marriage. And I didn't have the energy or the "want to" of going through all that hoopla that is part of what makes a wedding. Dress fittings and wedding showers and picking out flowers and deciding on who is in the wedding party? Bickering bridesmaids and drunk groomsmen? Just no. Absolutely not. No thank you with every fiber in my being.

Plus, we had both done the wedding thing before, and well . . . apparently, a wedding is not what a marriage makes.

And do I really know what makes a good marriage? No. But, from past experience, I can certainly tell you what doesn't. And from seeing many failed relationships with family and friends, I can certainly tell you what doesn't.

Allowing a job to take precedence over your marriage commitment will eventually cause hurt feelings. Spending more time with the kids than with your better half means someone is going to start feeling insignificant. Confiding in someone other than your best friend on life matters will ensure trust will be lost and arguments will be had. I'm not smart enough to know any of these things, in fact, can kill a marriage. But they're a darn good start.

There is only one thing allowed to stand between the two of us. Everything else takes a backseat. Nothing else matters. The one thing that stands between us is the very thing that holds us together: our faith in God.

So many times, it's been said marriage takes work. Okay, maybe for some it does. Probably for Keith, it does. For me? Not so much. It's been pretty effortless so far. For me. Heaven knows I can't speak for him. Don't get me wrong, we have our share of rough spots. There are days I alone am the roughest of all existing rough spots to him. Like a walking scrap of sandpaper. But I'm finding the more I keep God between us, the easier it is to put Keith's happiness above mine. And the easier it is to not see every single flaw the man has. And in doing that, my happiness soars. Any flaws he may have are insignificant on the scheme of things.

It's become not very difficult to consider him first in situations, and in turn, I find myself feeling as though I'm put first. It sometimes feels like a game. Or, for me, a competition. I've said many times, "I may not be athletic, but I'm darn sure competitive." And boy do I mean that. Without realizing it, we seem to try to outdo each other. Meaning, I think to have him a cold beer after work, and before I know it, my feet get a good rub before bed. I put a little extra effort toward supper and cook his favorite meatloaf and mashed potatoes, and the dishes are miraculously done before I finish my shower. Then there are those times the world hates me and I hate the world. And with no questions asked, a glass of chardonnay mysteriously appears by my chair while I'm plotting the demise of the universe, and I get a little quiet time to myself.

I know a lot of this might sound ridiculously old fashioned to some, and Heaven knows I know a lot about nothing when it comes to relationships of any kind, but it works for us. We had to find our groove. Our comfort zone. Our own little corner of the world. Once we did, we discovered we weren't just a husband and a wife living under the same roof. No . . . we are best friends. Best friends who can have just as much fun doing nothing together as we can two-stepping around a sawdusty dance floor. Best friends who are perfectly content being just us.

As I've gotten a little older, I've come to agree that life isn't always a party. It's not supposed to be. There is a lot of good to be found in contentment. That word was always the equivalent of boredom to me. Kinda blah. Nothing fancy. Plain. But let me tell you, there are days nothing feels more comfortable than that old contentment. Just like that old pinned-together bra. Or those old ragged tennis shoes. They just fit. They know you and they're like old friends who just feel good.

So back to my question of *you know when you know that you just know?* Yes . . . now, I know. And I surprise myself to see I know about more than I originally thought.

EPHESIANS 4:2-3

Be completely humble and gentle.
Be patient, bearing with one another in love.
Make every effort to keep the unity of the Spirit
through the bond of peace.

• CHAPTER 3 •

IF YOU CAN'T SAY SOMETHING NICE, DON'T SAY ANYTHING AT ALL IS WHAT I ALWAYS SAY, AND THAT'S GOOD ENOUGH.

Ever wanted to feel not good enough?

Ever hoped to live with someone who thinks they know more than you ever will?

Ever had the desire to sense you're just really not that smart?

Ever wanted to pray so much you were certain God was beginning to tune you out like a staticky radio station?

Then, if you're single, I suggest you go out and find yourself a man with a teenage daughter.

And then you marry him.

"Right this way, ladies, right this way! Don't be afraid! Step right up! Get your very own *I know everything there is to know about life and you don't* teenager right here! Get 'em while they last! Ladies, your circus is about to begin!"

When you marry a man who already has a teenage girl in his life, you're looking for a fight. Whether you realize it or not. It doesn't matter how nice you try to be or how fair you try to play. You're head down and butt up looking for a fight. For a fight, you aren't even sure how to fight, much less win. A fight you're uncomfortable dealing

34

with. A fight you really are too old for. No matter what your age is.

"My dad hates the way you cook."

"Why do you wear your hair like that? And why so much makeup?"

"Stop telling me I make you proud. I do what I do for me, not you."

"You're here for him, not me. I don't need you."

"You tell me you love me too much."

And the best part? All of this has been said more than once in a calm, controlled manner. As if it just came naturally. By someone who's goal in life is the perfect selfie.

I'm not sure if I wouldn't recommend dealing with a jealous ex-girlfriend instead. I tend to think that might be easier. Make your choice wisely.

I've always felt I was pretty darn good at letting crap and mean stuff people say just bounce right off of me. But there's one thing I've learned:

Words that soak into your soul are whispered . . . not yelled.

You can yell and scream at me all day long, and that garbage is gonna bounce right off. Sticks and stones, darling . . . sticks and stones. But simply say the words with a peaceful tone? That is gonna stick like butter and honey to my biscuit.

And I don't think for one minute that you mommas out there don't already hear this kind of stuff from your own teenaged daughters. Go ahead, laugh. I would if I were you. But let me tell you . . . it's pretty hard to stomach words like this coming from a child you didn't carry for nine months or a toddler you didn't cradle in your arms at the most hideous hour of the night because they couldn't sleep. Or a preschooler you didn't strap a little pink helmet on and teach how to ride a bicycle. Or a kindergartner you haven't kissed the skinned knee of. Because they were crying and calling for you: Mom.

No, this brand-new mom of a teenager stuff should come in a bottle. A medicine prescription bottle with a label. With all the side effects listed:

May cause nausea, diarrhea, vomiting

Inability to breathe at times
Occasional burning eyes
Intermittent ignorance
Unexplained outbursts
Excessive eye rolling
Regular gritting of teeth
Constantly repeating yourself
Constantly repeating yourself
Constantly repeating yourself

Let me start from what I know as her beginning.

In his mid-twenties, my husband was married to a woman for about ten years. During that marriage, she became addicted to prescription drugs, which eventually led to much harder stuff, as well as infidelity. As usually the case is. He became a police officer during that marriage, and much to his surprise, he'd get to proudly wear that uniform while bailing his wife out of jail. More than three times.

And taking her to rehab.

More than four times.

And don't think you're going to ask anything I didn't.

How did you, as a cop, not know what she was doing right there in your own house?

How did you not suspect anything?

Oh my Lord . . . weren't you so embarrassed? I mean, when you wallow with pigs, you gotta know you're gonna get dirty!

He's answered those questions and many more from me. As I'm sure you can imagine. And it seems like when unsavory things are happening right under your nose, you either don't see it . . . or you choose to not see it.

If you acknowledge it, then you gotta do something. Am I right?

And I guess I can understand that. I mean, in my first marriage, I kinda knew my husband was not being as faithful as Mother Teresa. Oh, who am I kidding? The neighbor's cat I threw rocks at was more faithful than he was. But if I acknowledged it, then I'd have a fight on my hands. And who had time for that? And what if I was wrong? But what if I was right? And where would I go? What would I do? What would my family think? Maybe if I just did nothing and turned the other cheek, it'd all go away.

Anyway, just as he was contemplating divorce, she became pregnant.

A brown-eyed, five-pound thirteen-ounce, seventeen-inch-long, curly-haired baby girl.

He was certain this was the answer to steer his wife straight and turn their marriage around. To get her on the right path. To take her attention off the drugs. And for the most part, in the very beginning, he said he felt that was exactly what was happening. But when he came home that one evening from a long day on the job, and the baby was in the same clothes she slept in the night before and an unchanged diaper, and her mother was passed out on the sofa, he knew it was time to go. That was the last straw. She could hurt him and cause him pain, but he could not allow her to hurt this baby.

Cayla was eighteen months old.

He filed for divorce.

After a year of back and forth with attorneys and custody disagreements and such, she walked away. She asked him for $1,500 and the title to his boat, handed the baby over, then simply walked away. Forever.

So now he had no boat, but he did have his baby girl. And all that baby girl had was her daddy.

Rejected by her mother.

My parents have been married for over fifty years, so I have no idea what it's like to not know one of them. Though I will admit, during my coming-of-age years, I would have sold my soul to have not known my mother. And not have to hear her ridiculous questions of where was I going and who would I be with and did I unload the dishwasher? And then she'd want to know about that pile of dirty clothes on the floor. And the bathroom . . . she'd harp on me about cleaning the bathroom. You know, all that caring stuff moms throw out there. I see now all that mess of questions was just mom lingo for, *I love you so much I care.*

So that was her beginning.

Now, here is my beginning.

My first marriage happened when I was twenty-three years young. Though I now see I was just a dumb baby, I genuinely thought I had it all together. My humor and my outlook on life were bright. This guy might not have been exactly what I was dreaming of in a man, but he was kinda nice to others, made a good living, and wanted children. And, well, he might not always have shown it, but he did tell me he loved me. So surely that meant something, right?

If I had any kind of real smarts, I would have immediately noticed he treated me nothing like my daddy treated my momma. Or my granddad treated my grandmother. Or even how Rhett treated Scarlett. And nothing like all that real love stuff you see in the movies that really isn't real love, but it's a movie, so come on.

But I knew best. So down the aisle I went.

A few years after getting all settled into a young married life, the days started to feel a bit humdrum, and the desire to hear little feet running through the house was growing strong. One year of trying to conceive turned into three years. The word "infertile" was being mentioned more times than I cared to count at doctor visits.

The bottom line? I cannot have children.

Rejected by God.

So, after hearing that and then enduring a year or three of his infidelity, I called it quits. It was all just too much.

Surely all these years later, my finding Keith, who had a daughter with no mother, must have been God's way of giving me another chance at this motherhood stuff, right? And His way of giving Cayla a chance at having a mother, right?

Really? Now that's funnier than a one-legged cat burying a turd on a frozen pond.

This has been the hardest job I've ever endured. I'm not sure I've ever prayed as much. Or shaken my fist at God so much. Or questioned Him so much. Or doubted Him.

I refuse to believe I wanted more than most other women in the world when it came to children. To simply be a good mother. To have a child that loved her, cried for her, laughed with her, hid from the world in her. A child she could teach, nurture, instill values and morals, raise up to love God and others. Why was this plea so difficult for God to understand?

So, when I met Keith . . . I just knew not only was he an answered prayer, but so was Cayla. She was like a big, giant bonus. I would have the family I had dreamed of and prayed for . . . but would I be good enough?

Once Keith and I married, the first year or so of family life was heaven. We were living in high cotton. We all three just fit. We clicked. We were good together. It felt like it was always meant to be.

I looked forward to sitting in dark school auditoriums clapping for her choir concerts. I excitedly cheered for her while she ran the bases at her softball games. I eagerly offered to drop her off with a hug at slumber parties.

Cayla and I were a great little team. Lots of weekend lunches out while her dad worked. We did movies, plenty of shopping, pedicuring and manicuring, just tons of girl stuff. We bought bras. We bought boots. We bought time together. She was beginning to feel like the daughter I never birthed. It was like she was always in my heart, just not in my life. It just took me a little while to find her. That *something is missing I'm just not sure what* hole in my heart was being filled. It was actually overflowing.

And then like that great pair of heels you just can't live without? The newness began to wear off. Blisters were starting to form. Family life was beginning to get, well, hard.

Just peachy.

And that right there is some sarcasm at its best.

Cayla was a full-fledged, thriving teenage girl now. Which meant doors were being slammed. Unsolicited biting comments flowed daily. Her bedroom reeked of feet and dirty hair. And her bathroom? Please. I wouldn't bathe a filthy sow in there. Chores constantly were forgotten if not purposely left undone.

Lots and lots of eye rolling and even more loud sighs. Lots. From me. Nothing was ever good enough for her.

Not even supper.

I was not good enough.

I couldn't figure out what happened. It's like one minute life was grand and the next minute I sucked. No more lunches out, movies started dwindling away, and my life had become one big fog. It was beginning to feel as if I had outstayed my welcome. And here in the South, we always say, *After a little time, fish and house guests start to stink.*

I pleaded for kindness. No more huffing and puffing. No more tolerating looks. I just wanted to have a peaceful living arrangement. I wanted us to work together. After over an hour commute home from sitting in a cubicle for eight grueling hours then standing in line at the grocery store, the absolute last thing I wanted to come home to were an attitude and a dirty kitchen to clean before I could even think about starting supper.

Then there was the day I was informed *we* don't use the dishwasher. It's a waste of electricity. Like she paid the bill or something.

"Dad and I always washed the dishes by hand before you got here. We never used the dishwasher."

We? Who was this *we* she spoke of? Was I not part of this *we*? I'd never met this so-called *we*, but if this *we* washed the dishes? *We* was my new best friend.

Well, it seemed *we* were nowhere to be found because on most days, there were always dirty dishes in the sink. I looked and looked for *we* but never was able to locate *we*. I was willing to pay *we* top dollar just so I could come home to an empty sink. But to no avail, I had no such luck. Cereal bowls, dirty spoons, and glasses with month-old rings in them from being left in her room for so long lovingly stretched out their arms to me from that sink almost every evening. So I put my foot down and explained that I might be a lot of things, but a maid I was not. And the dishwasher was then used. Heavily.

It seemed my feelings were always being beaten up on. I was beginning to get tired of feeling not good enough, and I didn't want to toughen up as Keith suggested. And Keith, God love him, he tried to explain to me it's just the way teenagers are. They can seem spiteful and mean, but it's just their way of pushing through life, and he was certain whatever she said, she didn't mean it intentionally. I didn't care, though. There's no good reason for feelings to ever be hurt, and, well, when someone tells you that you hurt them, you don't get to decide you didn't.

Okay, maybe in hindsight, I was becoming a mom. I mean, nothing I did was good enough or right enough or anything enough. She found fault with the way I cooked, the way I cleaned, the way I breathed. I was infringing on her time. Her way of doing things. Her household rules. She was there before me and figured she'd be there long after me. It was becoming a struggle as to who was the queen. And as I'd told Keith more than once, "The day she contributes more than a smelly room and a pissy attitude to this family, then and only then can she make any rules. But as long as my time, money, and energy was being used up to make her existence much like royalty . . . I am the 'Queen.'"

Besides, I don't know of any queens who rule a successful land and sleep till noon in a smelly room with clothes piled knee-high.

I did my best to referee the two of them when their sparks started to fly. And boy did their sparks fly. Keith has the patience of Job. Or more like four Jobs. But when he reached his limit, the sparks would fly. And his meeting place? The garage. I always knew when he looked at her with that look and pointed to the garage door . . . they would be having a *come to Jesus* meeting. But in the garage, of all places? I always felt Jesus deserved better.

I also did my best to keep the peace and support Keith the best I could.

"Please lower your voice and do not speak to your dad in that tone."

I also did my best to reward her for doing her chores or keeping her area of the house in order. Or at least for just doing something a little more than breathing.

"If you clean your room and get the clothes off the floor, we'll go get pedicures."

Because you catch more flies with honey than vinegar, right?

In other words, I did my best to be the best mom I could be. Or at least what I thought a best mom was. If nothing else, just good enough. However, that was about as appreciated as tits on a bull.

In hindsight, I should have done what every other good, God-fearing southern woman does with her family: scream and curse.

Shut your mouth and quit being ugly! Get in your room and get that dump cleaned up or you'll regret your next breath! And if you don't believe me, you're gonna have hell to pay!

But if you can't say something nice, don't say anything at all is what I always say, and that's good enough.

I mean, it worked with my mom. We all turned out okay. None of us are in a prison chain gang or making license plates now, are we? Looking back, my mom probably didn't scream and curse enough at us. And honestly, if it wasn't for us three girls, my mom probably wouldn't have screamed and cursed at all. Come to think of it, she should thank us for the colorful language we encouraged her to learn.

And speaking of my mom, I will never understand how or why she did it. I'm sure I gave her much more grief than I ever received. Though not a week passed I didn't hear, "Look at me like that again and I'll slap you into next week," and, "You better stop that fussing, or I'll give you something to fuss about, young lady!" I always knew her level of seriousness by whether or not "young lady" was tacked on to her threat. And it was tacked on quite a bit.

Anyway, I'm no saint. Not even close. For the love of all things fiery bright red, I'm a natural-born, purebred redhead. So, needless to say, there were more than a few times I lost my cool with my little family and barked and yelled and probably threw a sailor or two into cardiac arrest over the words coming out of my church-going mouth. But I do remind myself daily that the best sermons are lived and not preached. I just don't listen to myself daily.

A daughter. The very thing I prayed for, for so many years, was the very thing to cause me such heartache. I can't count how many times I would talk to me out loud and tell me, "I can't do this anymore," and, "This isn't what it's supposed to be like," and, "Why am I not good enough?"

And listen, if I'm honest with you, as different as Cayla and I are, we're very much alike.

I eventually realized neither of us wants to be hurt again. Or reminded of just how we don't have the very thing we feel we should have. Her? A mom. And me? A daughter.

It would be so much easier for me if she just wasn't lovable. If she was ugly acting to me. If she was disrespectful. If she was a complete heathen. But she's not. She's not any of that. She's been nothing more than a typical teenage girl doing what they do best: being a typical teenage girl.

For the most part, she's always been pretty awesome. Better than a lot of other kids I know, for sure. She'd never been a problem at school. Her grades continually skyrocketed. Heck, she graduated college in three years, with honors and two degrees. Her choices are stellar. Her compassion for others is bountiful. Her affection flows freely. At her core, she is the definition of joy. Simplistic joy.

I've come to see she doesn't know how to accept the advantages of having a mother's love. And am I even good enough to be the one to fill that void, anyway? No matter how painful it is for me who simply wanted to be good enough for her, there is no sin in that.

Now, let me tell you, I didn't barge into this family cracking a whip. I never wanted to be the one to discipline. Or the one to set the rules. Or the one to even enforce the rules. I'm a rule breaker, anyway. I simply wanted to feel included. To be part of the family. To feel good enough. To be the one who was called upon when that best friend betrayed her. To be the one to have long talks with about boys. To be the one she turned to when she didn't feel her best. It was too late for painting toenails and trimming bangs, but I would be more than fulfilled with the other stuff. I didn't know how to be a mother any more than she knew how to have a mother. I just assumed we'd learn together. I assumed I'd be good enough. And I assumed over time, it would all come naturally.

But you know what? It didn't. And for the most part, it still doesn't. There's not a whole lot of "natural" to be found when two people are playing roles they're not quite sure how to play. And we all know life isn't a dress rehearsal.

Over the years, there have been prom dresses bought. There's been heels stumbled in. There's been lipstick smudged. I've gone up against her daddy on her behalf to let her stay out past curfew. Let her go to that party. Let her push the envelope. Hoping this would make her like me or, Heaven forbid, maybe even love me. Or just be good enough.

Sometimes, it worked; most of the time, it didn't. Each day was a new day, and I never knew what to expect.

However, amongst all those negative comments and harsh words I've had hurled at me, I've had my hand held each Sunday in church during her years before leaving for college. Once, I even received flowers for Mother's Day. I've been given an abundance of cards for birthdays. Christmas has brought small plaques of love that read, *I love you to God and back*. And when she didn't know I was around, I overheard the words, "She has more faith than anyone I know, and it's because of her I've started doing a daily devotional and reading my Bible."

Once she left for college, I hoped we'd miss each other and somehow, over the miles, grow closer. Even if only by phone. Distance usually does a family well. And well, muddy water is best cleared by leaving it alone, right? And I suppose in some ways, we have grown a bit closer. There was that time I was invited to join her for a "Moms Weekend" with her sorority. I'm pretty sure she simply didn't want to be the only daughter there without a mom and have to explain. So I was basically the understudy. But that's okay, and it's more than enough for me. It was a great honor. However, it was the very first time I heard her say the words, "This is my mom," when introductions were made. I tried not to get sappy. It didn't work. I sobbed alone in the restroom.

And then many months later, there was that text. That text that came out of the blue one quiet morning. Expected never in this lifetime. Not from her to me, anyway. The one that made me question my sanity even harder. And it came the very day after I pitched a slight hissy fit because I was feeling like a nobody who mattered to no one in this family. Nobody cared about my opinion. Nobody wanted my advice. Nobody cared. Woe is me, huh? My knickers were in a knot tighter than they had ever been knotted.

This text that I received? It thanked me for loving her father so well. For being such a good wife to him. And to know I did not go unnoticed and the gratefulness she had for such a role model as me.

And that she loved me.

Oh, and the very one who caused me so much heartache? Get this. She was the very one to give me the best gift I've ever received.

On my fiftieth birthday.

And it all started with a simple text.

"Hey, I mailed your gift, and I just called your post office. They said it's there. It's perishable, so you need to go get it now, so it doesn't spoil! Sorry for the late notice!"

I had thirty minutes to get to a post office that was forty-five minutes away.

Somehow, I made it. And I ran to the front doors, pushed them open, and there was my gift.

Cayla.

With a huge smile.

Holding flowers.

Standing in the post office.

Giggling.

It was the biggest, most precious surprise of my whole fifty years.

Yes, she got me. She got me good. Now, I've gotta up my game. I've said it before, I may not be athletic, but I'm darn sure competitive.

She drove for eight hours. For me. For my birthday. For her mom.

That birthday weekend was a gift of manicuring and pedicuring and lunching and laughing and girl talking.

It was a gift of joy. Simplistic joy.

For the first time in my life, I was a mom.

For the first time in my life, I had a daughter.

For the first time in my life, I was good enough.

And it is times like these I am quite sure I am nothing more than three gallons of crazy in a two-gallon bucket.

And it is also times like these I know God must've been bored and figured He'd do some good old-fashioned knee slappin' at my expense.

Watching her flourish away at college has brought me some proud moments. Sure, she's made the president's list. Sure, she's held a job. Sure, she's active in her church college group. But whatever. It's the way she keeps her room spotless. Like she saw me do when she was at home. How she makes her bed each morning. Like she saw me do when she was at home. Seeing her car sparkling clean when she's in for a visit. Like she saw mine was when she was at home. That perfect shade of lip gloss. Like mine. That flawless face of makeup. Oh, and the heels . . . the cute and sassy heels she has. You get it.

Growing up with a teenager I didn't raise from birth is quite possibly the toughest path I've ever walked. And never more in my life have I felt more alone than when on that path. And I do believe I'm the one who is doing the "growing up" here. I'm having to learn to take what comes and either soak it in or let it bounce off. And there's never any hints or clues as to which is best at the time. I will say for me, it's not been all that easy. Half the time I don't know if I should scratch my butt or wind my watch, for Heaven's sake.

I do see, though, every path in life will always have a few puddles. Some puddles are much deeper than others. But they will all be passable. None too deep to wade through. None too wide to go around. But there will be puddles. Those puddles will be the very thing that makes you yearn for the fresh, dry land. And keep in mind, some of those puddles will ruin that great pair of heels, too. You have to determine which puddles to walk through and which puddles to walk around.

So, for any of you who want to be a momma but maybe can't be a momma or aren't sure how to be a momma and are unsure you can even be a good enough momma?

Do it.

Even if you don't carry them for nine months . . . do it. I'm not gonna lie, though. It's hard. It's a giant pain in the *you know what times twenty* when you're awake. It can be a never-ending feeling of not being good enough. But you know what? You are. You are good enough. If no one else ever tells you, I will. You are good enough. You're actually better than good enough.

Why? Because "good enough" is there because she wants to be, not because she has to be. "Good enough" doesn't walk away when it's the easier thing to do. "Good enough" stands firm and pushes through, even when curling up in a corner seems like the better option. "Good enough" sacrifices. Time, energy, money, tears, you name it, it's sacrificed. "Good enough" struggles with unanswered prayers, sanity, dirty dishes, feeling left out, and I could go on and on. "Good enough" sits in the shadows while everyone else gets the credit and the hugs. "Good enough" cries. A lot. And then a little more. "Good enough" prays, because for the most part, that's where any and every answer, if there is one, can be found.

"Good enough" is simply more than enough.

This *taking on a teenager you didn't birth* can pull up past resentments. It can cause lots of anger. It can cause a tremendous amount of heartache. It can make you feel less than the bottom of the barrel.

But, then, there are a lot of things it teaches you. It teaches you how to be patient. How to be kind and not envious. It shows you how you should never boast or be proud. It shows you how to protect your heart, trust in God, never give up hope, and to continuously forge ahead.

I do believe I've finally come to realize my finding Keith who had a daughter with no mother was God's way of teaching me I am actually good enough. Even if I'm the only one who thinks so at times. And I also believe this is God's way of keeping me close to Him. And leaning on Him. And depending on Him. And talking with Him.

And His way of making me see that my joy must be rooted in simplicity.

Simple words. Simple expressions. Simple thoughts. Simple actions.

This is my mom.

Thank you for loving my dad.

She has more faith than anyone I know.

You do not go unnoticed.

I love you.

Because words that soak into your soul are whispered . . . not yelled.

And that, my sweet friend . . . will forever be absolutely good enough. For both of us.

PSALM 139:14

I praise you, for I am fearfully and wonderfully made.
Wonderful are your works; my soul knows it very well.

• CHAPTER 4 •

IF ANYTHING IN LIFE CAUSES YOU TO BOW UP LIKE A BANTY ROOSTER, IT'S BEST TO JUST WALK AWAY.

Glancing back over life, and I say "glancing" because down here in the South, we're taught it's not nice to stare, I see that I fall somewhere between Scarlett O'Hara from *Gone with the Wind*:

"Great balls of fire. Don't bother me anymore!"

And Ouiser Boudreaux from *Steel Magnolias*:

"Shut up."

And the older I get, it seems Ouiser is wanting to take the lead. A strong lead.

And I'm just fine with that. Both women are strong-willed, persistent, full of spirit, a little rugged in their own way, and charmingly venomous.

Scarlett just seemed to always be perfectly intact. Very well put-together. In vogue. A fashion plate, some might say.

And Ouiser? Why, her coffee tastes much better with an extra splash of profanity and a hard eyeroll to the left while stirring it with her middle finger.

The only thing I noticed that neither of these ladies did much of that we do a lot of down here in the South?

Smile.

Yes, that's what we do down here in the South. We smile.

A lot.

I've been told more times than I can count that the older a woman becomes, the more she likes herself. The more she appreciates the struggles she's endured. The more her confidence in herself begins to soar. The more she cares about what she thinks rather than the *thinks* of others.

And something else that's pretty cool about becoming an older woman? She has the wisdom to know.

She may not always know what she knows. But she does just know.

She starts to realize that she knows herself. Or at least that's how it was for me. I guess that's what it means when we hear in books and movies, "She found herself." She discovers she knows what she wants and when she wants it. She is no longer worried about if she's in style or not. Because in her mind, she never went out of style. She has her own style. And no one else can duplicate or devastate her style. Because it's hers and hers alone. It's who she is.

And she's proud of it.

She has her own style in everything. Not in just her heels and hairstyle. But in her character. Her morals. Her standards. Her faith. Her loyalty. Her newfound boldness.

There's not a whole lot of deep thinking about things or asking girlfriends for their *not really needed or really wanted for that matter* opinions. The older she gets, the less she cares about what most anyone else thinks. The opinions of others have mattered far too much in her past decision making, anyway.

However, I do think the one important thing a woman comes to know the older she gets? Her worth.

She knows her worth. And if she's a strong, bold woman from the South, she'll add tax.

And I do believe it's true. You finally realize who you really are.

And for many of us, it's the first time we actually start to accept ourselves for who we are.

Or at least that's how it is for me. The older I get, the more I like me. The real me. The me who shows up and seldom shuts up.

After looking back over all these years, I think life would have been just a tad bit easier if we were always just "real" with who we are. If we just owned up to our true selves. If we always just said what we meant and felt how we felt, out loud, for the whole world to hear, rather than smothering our ideas and our opinions on things because, well, somebody else might not like it. Instead, there are so many times I would church it up and fancy up my thoughts and feelings to satisfy everyone else. Because Heaven forbid I hurt someone's feelings. Regardless of how many times they hurt mine. And now? I can't for the life of me understand why I did that.

And don't get me wrong. I'm not suggesting for a minute that we should ever walk around barking orders and being rude or inconsiderate to others. For Heaven's sake, no way. But I do think there are kind ways to say anything and considerate ways to do anything without bullying and simply being barbaric.

I mean, why do we pretend to be someone we're not? Someone God didn't intend for us to be? Someone who works at being someone they're not?

And like I always say, "God can't bless who you pretend to be."

I have discovered over the past few years that I really like me. The real me. Now, I may not be proud of me every waking minute, but I do like me. The me who may, or may not, have unapologetically had that bowl of leftover mac and cheese for breakfast. The me who may, or may not, have had that glorious glass of wine alone. The me who may, or may not, have said those words that should never leave a southern girl's churchgoing mouth. Words that were uttered right there, on a Sunday morning, in the church parking lot.

The me who tolerates just so much then shrugs it off and walks away. With a smile.

Because, yes, that's what we do down here in the South. We smile. A lot.

Listen to this. I remember that time I went to purchase my first car. I was in my mid-forties. And I say it was my first car because that's precisely what it was: *my* first car. No other name on the title . . . just me and the bank. No daddy and no husband. Just me.

I did my research, so I knew what I wanted. From make, model, exterior color, interior color, how many doors, etc. Actually, if I'm honest, that research consisted of my seeing the car parked outside a hotel while I was out of town for work. I saw it and instantly knew. Kinda like when I met Keith for the first time. I saw him and instantly knew. I just knew. This was the one. I just didn't kiss the car there at our first meeting. There was no dating other cars or playing the field. This was it. My in-depth research was done.

Once I financially decided what my bank told me I could afford, off I went to the car dealerships.

Standing in the heat, on asphalt I just knew would start bubbling under my freshly pedicured toes glistening with polish to die for, it didn't take long before I heard myself utter the words, "There she is. That's the one. That one right there." Standing in the perfectly organized car dealership lot with cars somehow puzzle parked so close together I had to suck it in to squeeze a look in the window, Keith flipped his head around and gave out a rather interested, "Oooohhh." It sounded as if he had just received a complimentary gym membership where he didn't have to actually go to the gym but somehow bulked up anyway. While eating fistfuls of Oreos.

And you know, down here in the South, we "suck it in" when we want our midsection to appear smaller and our chest to appear broader. Sucking it in applies to both men and women. Like when you're at the beach and that heartthrob is walking your way. You suck it in. Or when we just need to squeeze past something placed hideously too close to something else.

You just sucked it in, didn't you?

Me, too. And on that note . . . I need another glass of wine.

Anyway, perfectly coiffed and suavely perched right next to my newfound monthly commitment mysteriously appeared none other than the almighty, well-suited car salesman.

"She's a beaut."

A beaut?

Who says that? Other than out of the mouth of a car salesman, I've never heard that term used before.

You know, I'd be willing to bet that has to be the first term any car salesman must conquer before hitting the lot.

After introductions in weather that was quickly becoming hotter than a two-dollar pistol at the local pawn shop, the small talk commenced. And we were strolling around what I was sure to be my new mode of transportation. And we strolled for what seemed like a two-mile lap in that heat. Then we were sitting in it, starting it up, fiddling with the radio, moving the seat forward and backward, opening the sunroof, and I was telling Keith to stop messing with the seat warmers because my tush was starting to sweat.

Then lo and behold, that coveted test drive was offered.

But no way, no how. I was not having it. I was no fish swimming around a hook with an expensive four-door bait dangling on it, just jiggling around trying to get my attention so I'd bite. If that happened, I was stuck. I was hooked. It was going to be all but impossible to get away. And then my lip was gonna hurt.

Upon my third smiling and once again saying, "Thank you, but I don't think so," to a test drive, we were invited inside to discuss our options. Our options. Ours. And let's be honest, *I* was the only *our* here with any options. And there were basically only two options: to either find me making a monthly note on this particular "beaut" . . . or not. I'm not one for playing games and I'm not one for being bullied, and I do know my boundaries. So, let's discuss.

While sitting tall and confident in the salesman's office, daintily sipping that lukewarm water I was offered in that little plastic cup that I secretly hoped hadn't just been recycled at my expense, I was ready to talk.

The salesman proceeded to take out some paper, peck around on his calculator, make a few odd stares and facial contortions at whatever he just wrote on that paper, scratch his chin, then look at Keith, who he respectfully referred to as "Mr. Kinnard."

It was then a few questions were tossed his way. Mr. Kinnard's way, that was. He asked the typical questions, such as, "Will there be a trade-in?" and, "About where are you wanting to be, dollar wise, on your note each month?" and other questions of that nature.

Again, sitting tall and confident, I patiently listened. Mr. Kinnard was looking a little bit nervous, and his eyes kept darting from the salesman to both my highly raised eyebrows and smile. Before my eyes, he appeared to develop a rather glowing forehead. If this was some girlfriend sitting with me, I would have suggested she slap some powder on that blindingly shiny brow. Or to at least lean forward so I could check my lip gloss in that glistening noggin. However, it wasn't. So I just smiled and counted his nervous stutters. There's one. There's another. And another.

Finally, Keith looked at me, leaned my way, and quietly asked, "Do you have any thoughts on any of this?" That was when the salesman excused himself to go speak to his manager about where we were on things.

We. Like he was a part of this purchase.

"Oh, I have thoughts. I have plenty of thoughts. Here's one thought for you: I'm about to bow up like a banty rooster in here if he continues to talk directly to you only, Mr. Kinnard."

Emphasis on *Mr. Kinnard*.

Keith slid back in his chair, closed his eyes, interlocked his fingers, and appeared to be praying. I did not interrupt. His time with the Lord is important to me.

By the way, a banty rooster, or bantam, is about one-fourth the size of a regular chicken. They're bred for cockfighting. Which was quickly becoming where I was going.

And, rumor has it, if anything in life causes you to bow up like a banty rooster . . . it's best to just walk away.

Upon his return, the salesman told us what the best his manager said they could do on this deal was, turned his little piece of scrawled-on paper toward Keith, then pushed it across the table. Directly in front of Mr. Kinnard. I then obnoxiously leaned over to get a glimpse of just what was on that paper.

I leaned over. I did. Me. The purchaser of this *beaut* that the salesman and Mr. Kinnard were discussing.

And I smiled.

Because yes, that's what we do down here in the South. We smile. A lot.

And in my softest, most delicate ladylike tone I could controllably muster at that moment, they heard:

"That's not going to work for me. But I do appreciate your time, sir, and will get back in touch with you should I change my mind."

That salesman's head snapped my way quicker than a squirrel dodging a Buick on a backcountry road. Mr. Kinnard folded his hands, placed them quite gracefully over his forehead and eyes, and slumped down in his chair. Praying again, I supposed. Like I said, his time with the Lord is important to me and, well, I do love a man who loves the Lord.

I pierced the salesman's eyes with my smile.

"Well, ma'am, this is the best we can do in this situation. Now, Mr. Kinnard, if you'd like to consider maybe a trade-in, we could possibly go a different route."

I felt about as welcome at that desk as an outhouse breeze in the heat and humidity of a smoldering summer.

And "ma'am."

He said "ma'am." Not "Mrs. Kinnard" or "you redheaded imbecile." But "ma'am."

And let's not get me wrong. Manners play a big role in the upbringing of kids in the South. Hardly a day passed we didn't hear

Momma or Granny bark out, "Mind your manners, little lady!" We are taught to say "yes, sir" and "no, ma'am." If we are so inclined to be a little less formal, we can certainly address adults by their first name. But it sure better have Mr. or Mrs. in front of it or Momma would catch you by that thin little layer of skin on the back of your neck just under the hairline. With her freshly manicured and sharp fingernails. Ouch. Anyway, everybody knows you refer to someone as "ma'am" or "sir" when addressing them only if you can't remember their name. So, if Keith could be "Mr. Kinnard," then certainly I could be a little more than just "ma'am."

"Thank you, sir. And again, I do appreciate your time and will get back in touch with you should I change my mind."

Emphasis was on *sir*, of course.

I wanted to unleash my Ouiser at that point and just politely, yet not too politely, tell him to shut up. But then there are those manners. And hearing my momma in my head barking, "Mind your manners, little lady!" didn't help matters.

I think that was about when it was determined I had butted in on this conversation between the salesman and Mr. Kinnard about the car *I* was purchasing one too many times.

He teetered back in his cheaply upholstered chair and relaxingly placed both hands behind his head and gave a sigh. He did his best to appear unmoved. Then, nonchalantly, he asked, "Just who is actually making this purchase decision?"

Mr. Kinnard lifted his face up from behind his prayerfully folded hands that were attached to his slumped body and, with a look of surrender, simply stated, "She is."

And slowly pointed at yours truly.

He knew the salesman, as well as his commission, was doomed from that breath forward.

I sat straight up and gave a tilted head, doe-eyed smile to the salesman and said rather daintily, with maybe a tad bit of exaggerated southern sarcasm full of backwoods twang, "Yes. This is my purchase.

I will be the only one purchasing this vehicle, and it will be in my name alone. Just mine. No one else. Not even Mr. Kinnard's. Just little ol' me."

Keith continued to spend quiet time with the Lord while the now well-informed salesman jumbled his words, shuffled his papers, and awkwardly chuckled. Then, again, asked me just what it was I was looking for on this deal.

I then, while still smiling at the salesman, and in one clean jerk of the wrist, quickly slid the paper from in front of Keith to directly in front of me. Though I appeared to be studying the paper for a bit, I knew at this point my mind was made up. How? Because I just knew.

I was now just lollygagging around. Wasting time. Dragging my feet. Moving slower than molasses headed up a hill. I was not going to purchase anything from anyone who then felt I was the nuisance turd in the punchbowl and taking up too much of his day. He didn't seem to have the time to be dealing with *ma'am*. As far as I was concerned, he could just sit behind that cheap desk looking down his nose at me all day long. I was taking my own sweet time.

Actually, maybe I was being a bit of a nuisance. But I was a nuisance with money in my pocket. Or at least in an already approved account at my trusty bank. And I didn't see nary a soul standing in line behind me throwing greenbacks at his desk.

And anyway, he was rushing me. And every man with any amount of sense knows you do not rush a woman. The only thing worse than rushing a woman is attempting to baptize a cat. It ain't happening. She'll change her outfit for the eighth time. She'll re-do her hair. She'll call her momma. I will not be rushed, and he was attempting to rush me on a big decision that was solely my decision to make. And I don't know of anything in life meant to be rushed. Much less big money spending stuff.

After pretending like I was putting loads of thought into what was scribbled on this paper in front of me, I quickly slid it around to face him, and I jerkily pushed it back his way, stating, "No. No, thank you. But I do appreciate your time. Mr. Kinnard, I'm ready if you are."

I then pushed my chair back and stood.

Upon that silly little move, I heard, "Well, ma'am . . . this may just be a little too much car for you. And I can certainly understand that. Would you be interested in possibly looking at another model that is significantly lesser in price?"

It was as if the world went into slow motion at that very moment. You have no idea how almost impossible it was to not belt out Ouiser's, "Shut up."

It was like he was deaf in one ear and couldn't hear out of the other. How many times was I gonna have to politely smile and say, "No, thank you?"

And I kept reminding myself in my quiet voice that only I could hear screaming in my head, *Remember! There's a big difference between a southerner and a redneck, and you don't wanna be a redneck!* You see, southerners tend to stay calm with a smile and a soft touch of scathing contempt. Rednecks? Well, they just call up all the cousins. And, as luck would have it, I didn't have any cousins living around these parts, anyway.

As I was standing and placing my purse over my arm, it was then I swore I heard a loud thud. Either Keith fell over in prayer or his chin hit the floor. I wasn't sure which, and at the time, I did not care. Because now, I was eye to eye with that salesman. With both hands flat on that desk, leaning toward him and again smiling.

"Sir, I can assure you that car or any other car you have on your lot is certainly not too much car for me. And I do not appreciate your patronizing words. You, sir, are braver than the first man to ever eat an oyster, I will give you that. But as I've said already more than three times, I am not interested. However, I do appreciate your time. And thank you, sir."

Of course, all of that was a nice and fancied-up version of Scarlett's, "Great balls of fire. Don't bother me anymore!"

I was done. I was ready to drive out the same car I drove in. A blind man on a galloping horse could have seen that.

It was then I turned to walk away from this fool, and I was headed toward the door.

With no Keith.

Because he was somehow stuck in position at that desk just staring at me with utter disbelief on his sweet face. With my purse on my arm, I paused and slowly looked back at him. I motioned to him while giving him "that look." That look that he has yet, to this day, learned to understand as, *Get a move on!* Then I sternly yet quietly announced with somewhat clenched teeth and pursed lips, "I'm leaving. Are you coming with me or not?"

After all, I was the one with the keys.

I was going to tolerate just so much. It was then I walked away. With a smile.

Because again, that's what we do down here in the South. We smile. A lot.

I don't recall the salesman ever rising from his desk. And I don't recall hearing another "ma'am" escape his lips.

Two weeks later, I was the proud monthly note-maker of that exact vehicle's twin purchased without incident for a much better price than from where I did not purchase it in the first place.

And, I must say, that purchase was smoother than a hairy chest after wax day.

I knew within the first few seated minutes at that first salesman's desk this was not going to be a sale for his books. I knew. I just knew. And he probably knew, too.

But the second salesman? Simply charming. Manners that reached high heaven. His momma raised him quite well, if I should say so myself. Plus, the water he offered me came in a glass. With ice. And down here in the hot South, ice alone can make or break just about any deal.

Roll the tape back twenty years. There I was sitting at the first salesman desk. I would have had zero confidence in myself, and I would have hemmed and hawed and all but have begged him to sell me that car. And probably at a price I couldn't afford. Not today. Not going to happen. When it comes to me now, I call the shots. I make the decisions. Because I live with the outcome. I know what I want, and I know what I won't tolerate.

And Keith knew it, too. How, you ask? Well, remember back when we were just dating, and it was about as clear as a mud fence to me just where our relationship was going? So I made it quite clear that I was not going to be anyone's fifty-year-old girlfriend? I told him that because I wasn't playing around anymore. With anyone. And now? Well, I have the wisdom to know not to waste my time over anyone. Not even if they're holding the keys to a "beaut" that I am throwing my pristine, hard-earned credit at.

You see, I had hit the age where I was not going to be bullied or pushed or convinced about anything, and I absolutely recognized my boundaries.

You know, over the years, I may have gained a buttermilk biscuit or two around the hips, but I've also gained a whole lot of confidence in who I am. And also in who I was. And who I was yesterday taught me to be who I am today. Yesterday, I was what you might call a softy or a people pleaser. My peace of mind and my worth came after everyone else was taken care of. I put others first. Their feelings, their wants, and their needs. And the only things that really purchased me was a bad marriage, then a divorce, a bunch of heartaches, crashing self-esteem, a sense of no pride. Now? I like to think of myself first. I put me ahead of the rest. It's not always easy, and there are days I fail at it. Many days, now that I think about it. But I do my best.

And I don't mean I put myself at the front of the line in a selfish or egotistical sort of way . . . more of a *gotta protect my heart and my big assets* sort of way.

Listen, if you don't look out for you, who is? At the end of the day, you are the one left with your decisions and the choices you made. Good or bad. Right or wrong. And let me tell you, not every decision you make is going to be right. And not every choice you make is going to be fulfilling. But I promise you, if you take care of you, then you can weed through most of what life throws at you fairly easy. And then you'll have the wherewithal and the strength and the inner peace to take care of not only you but everyone else.

For, when you put yourself first, everybody wins. When you take care of yourself, everybody wins. When you love you, everybody wins.

The more gray hairs I squealed at, the faster wisdom came dashing in at breakneck speed, too. I have gained a bit of both, gray hair and wisdom, if I may say so myself. My, oh, my. If I only knew then what I know now!

I mean, a cat can have kittens in an oven, but that don't make 'em biscuits. And what I mean by that is you can sit your tush in church every Sunday morning, but that doesn't make you a saint. We might sometimes find ourselves looking down our freshly powdered nose at the neighbors, kinda like that salesman was doing me. But we don't always know why the neighbors are living like they are living, now do we? I've learned I now have enough wisdom to know that I don't always know what I think I know. And what I do know? Well, it ain't always the way it's presented.

You can bet, there are three sides to every story: Yours, theirs, and the truth. But I will be the first to admit, right or wrong, it's sometimes a bit fun to gawk at the neighbors. You just better know Jesus is watching. And he has an angel named Karma. And if you want an unexpected visit from Karma . . . just start pointing out the faults of others with your soft little manicured fingers. Karma will come a-knocking and sit for a visit. Usually longer than what you have time for. Trust me on this. I know. And she likes honey in her tea. Her sweet tea.

And when all that confidence and wisdom was being gained, that's when I discovered I respect me. I appreciate myself. I actually like myself. Cellulite, gray hair that I will forever color dark auburn, and all. I can do me better than anyone else can. I might tend to bark a little too loud some days. I might make no sense to anyone but me on others. I might say a few words the local church ladies would cringe at, but it's me. It's who I am. And I've finally accepted that. After years of trying to be who everyone else wanted me to be and do what everyone else wanted me to do and ending up never feeling quite up to par, this is as good as I get. And you can bet your last paycheck, you are getting my best.

My very best.

Whether it meets your expectations or not.

For my sweet daddy has always said, "Never let anyone define who you are or tell you your worth. That's only for you and life to decide."

And that has proven to be so true over time.

We eventually become confident appreciating the fact we have the wisdom to know our worth.

Never be ashamed of where you've been. Or where you've come from. Or what you've endured. You can't make the grade if you don't take the test. Be proud of your best achievements. Be pleased with those tough decisions you made. Be satisfied with the outcome of those trials you trudged through. Maybe they didn't all end up in your favor . . . but you endured. You fought the good fight, and you finished the race. Those worst mistakes you cringe to think about? That ex-husband, or that embarrassing side job, or that ridiculous investment you knew you shouldn't have made the very minute you made it? Be proud. If for no other reason than to know you will never make those blunders again.

But above everything else, don't be afraid.

Don't be afraid of what others think. Of what they might say. Of not being enough.

Just believe.

In yourself. In your faith. In your strength. In your wisdom. And most of all, in God's grace.

Life's greatest trials of yesterday have made us who we are today. Heartaches, headaches, and mistakes all play a huge part in who we are and where we're going.

And how we're going to get there.
And always remember . . . a smile.
Because that's what we do down here in the South. We smile.
And that, my friend, we do a lot.

PROVERBS 3:15

"Wisdom is more precious than rubies;
nothing you desire can compare with her."

CHAPTER 5

HAVING MORE GUTS IN LIFE THAN YOU CAN HANG ON A FENCE CAN BRING YOU MANY OF LIFE'S GREATEST BLESSINGS.

I t was a crisp, spring Saturday afternoon.

"I need to talk to you about something."

Oh, boy. This could only mean one of about a million things. He must've checked the credit card statement.

Or he somehow found out I don't really wear a "small." A small anything. Except for earrings. I do sometimes wear small earrings.

Oh, wait just a minute. I knew what it was. Some way or the other, he figured out I was actually choking down his last frozen mini Snickers last night when I garbled a yell back to him from the kitchen that we didn't have anymore.

You know, the only time those words can mean anything good for me is when it's God. When He's telling me, in my heart, He's got something we need to chat about. Something good. Something exciting. Something filled with joy.

And don't get me wrong. Keith is big in my book. Top of the food chain big. Cooler than the other side of the pillow. But let's be real . . . he ain't God.

"I've been toying with the idea of retiring."

Retiring . . . from what? Yard work? Carbs? Laughing at my not-funny jokes? Me? What was he talking about?

Apparently, the puzzled look of awe I shot his way helped him comprehend my lack of understanding. My lack of understanding this crazy talk that was spewing from his donut door, that is.

You see, Keith had been in law enforcement for, well, pretty much all of his entire adult life. Since his early twenties anyway, and now he was in his, well, not early twenties. Law enforcement, cop stuff, civil servant-ing, it was all he knew. His paw paw was a sheriff and an uncle was a police officer or something like that. And then I had a great uncle who was a police officer. Momma said he was shady, though. Stayed on the edge of what was and wasn't legal. Had to watch him like a hawk. But he doesn't really count since he's not on Keith's side of the family.

Anyway, in his early years, he transported hardened jailbirds from prison to prison. After that, he worked on death row. More than once, he'd been known to escort an inmate to his execution. The inmate's execution, that is.

Give me a minute here, but I remember not too long ago, he took me to visit the big prison where he worked in his beginnings. Huntsville, Texas. It was huge. Big fences with barbed wire everywhere. I saw a prison guy dressed in white outside mowing. I wanted to take a picture, but of course, Keith wouldn't let me. Said it was rude. Asked how I'd like it if that were me and people were driving by taking pictures.

"I'd smile and pose with the kids. Why?"

Anyway, we were in the museum of this insanely large prison, and I was reading all the stuff on the walls and ooohing and ahhing all the old photos on display. And as luck would have it, the now-retired warden that governed the prison back when Keith worked there was visiting, as well. Those two were chatting like old friends, reminiscing about old times, and I noticed their conversation and laughter was getting a tad loud for my likes. All I know is, from through the bookshelf where I was eavesdropping, I heard Keith belt out, "Man, things have sure changed since my time spent here!"

I about died. Actually, I'm sure for a brief bit of time, I did die. People were looking. Staring. Gawking, to say the least. They were probably thinking they were fish-eyeing the likes of Clyde. Which would make me Bonnie. I couldn't shut him up and get him out of there fast enough.

Anyway.

Keith had seen the worst of the worst in his career. He'd ticketed, he'd arrested, he'd jumped fences, he'd chased. He'd tased, he'd tackled, he'd testified, he'd pulled the trigger. All more times than I care to know.

However, there are many more instances where he'd been known to offer a hug. Reach into his pocket and give to those without. Convince a struggling veteran that life was worth one more day. He'd held the hand of a battered wife. He'd wiped the tear of a fatherless child. He'd prayed with the unexpected widow.

No way could he give it up now after well over twenty-five years. Was he nuts? Who was he gonna patrol, if not the citizens of this great county of ours?

Plus, I can't handle being under constant surveillance. I mean, he excels at reminding me to put on my seat belt. He does an exceptional job at constantly pointing out my excessive speed. He invariably reminds me the left lane is for passing. The left lane, not the left turn lane. And preferably pass just one car at a time . . . not seven. Without breaking a sweat, he argues my made-up scenarios of when I could, and should not, be allowed to legally shoot someone.

I'm fifty now, for Heaven's sake. And a redhead. In my mind, that's more than enough reasons to justify shooting anything.

Anything.

The man has received a Medal of Valor for a shootout he was in, as well as a Life Saving Award for saving some guy in a motorcycle accident. And if that ain't enough, he's been awarded Crime Prevention Officer of the Year, as well as numerous other awards that I should be ashamed to not know off the top of my head.

And, even though you didn't ask, he looks hot in his uniform. That, I do know.

Keith was the best of the best. Why give it up now?

So, being the supportive wife I am, I should probably support him as his supportive wife. So I asked a few questions I felt, as his supportive wife, I had the right to know.

"You wanna do what? Retire? You can't retire now! Are you out of your ever-lovin' mind? I'm only fifty. *What am I supposed to do*? Not sit in traffic for an hour each morning? No longer pray that my *way too tight* skirts will miraculously fit after not going to the gym like I say I do? Am I just supposed to sit around this house and do nothing? No more *way too long* conference room meetings listening to office folks yammer about crap they know nothing about? Should I just toss all of my *way too high* heels in the trash? They're not cheap, you know. What will I have to gripe about if I'm not gainfully employed? And what am I supposed to do about money? My retirement account 'might' get me through next month if I don't eat. What is going on up there in that head of yours? Did you meet another woman? Is that what this is about? You better start sleeping in that bulletproof vest of yours if this has anything to do with another woman . . . "

Take note: if whatever is taking place is not about me, I have a craft of somehow making it about me. It's an art. And a fine art at that, I might add.

He eventually was able to get a word in edgewise and shut me up for a brief moment.

You see, he can handle a criminal all right, but this is me we're talking about here. And he should already know by now letting this cat out of the bag is a lot easier than putting it back in.

"No, no, no. I didn't say *you* retire. I said me. And there's no other woman and you're not going to starve or throw away any shoes. I just thought I'd like to slow down a bit and actually enjoy life rather than continue to watch it blow by at breakneck speed."

Well, why didn't he just say that from the start? Why get me all riled up and sputtering like an old wet hen?

"Well, we're gonna have to talk about this. I mean, am I just supposed to get up and go to work while you sleep late each morning? Are you going to do the dishes, wash the clothes, cook the meals? I don't make enough to support me *and* this family. I mean, if a trip around the world costs a dollar, I couldn't even make it to the county line!"

I was then reminded he had a pension.

"Oh. Yeah. Well, that's nice and all, but what are you going to do all day? Take up knitting? Watch *The Young and the Restless*?"

Daddy always reminded me to make sure I load my brain before I shoot my mouth off, and I'd seemingly not yet learned that little gem.

That's when he broke the "new" news to me.

"Actually, I wanted to also talk to you about this other opportunity that has come up. It's with the state. The parks and wildlife division. They have an opening at Big Bend Ranch State Park for a police officer and, well, I've always liked that area. Remember, that's where we went on vacation last Christmas in the RV, and you loved it. So I'd still be working, but it would be much less stress and in such a peaceful place."

Questions with no possible answers were bouncing from temple to temple now, and I immediately knew there was no way this could possibly work. Not for me, anyway.

If I remembered correctly, that vacation we took after Christmas wasn't just down the road a piece. It took like three days to get there. That's a tad longer of a commute than I was interested in. I mean, I had eleven years invested with this company where I worked. I had lived in this city for close to fifteen years. This was home. How could I leave this city? Plus, I'd heard you live longer when you live in the city. But I know that's not true. It just feels like you do. But it was my city. And I finally felt like I had all my eggs mostly in one basket. You might even say I finally had a handle on life. Why would I give that up just to have to start over somewhere else? Nobody, especially me, likes being the "new girl" anywhere. Especially in some small border town.

I wasn't moving. Anywhere.

I did not get married just to make dates with my husband on weekends. I couldn't do that living apart stuff. I know that might work for some of y'all, but no. Not for me. Not happening. Not even gonna try it. I did that single girl stuff for close to ten years after my first marriage. And if I might say so myself, I was good at it. Swore I'd never get married again, then BOOM. Keith showed up in my life, made me get all lovestruck, created huge chaos in my heart, and then changed all the future plans that I made for me. And now that I was really loving married life and crazy about this man I call my hot husband, he wanted to up and move over . . . wait, let me check MapQuest . . . Oh my Lord! Over twelve hours away? *Are you kidding me?* And to the Texas/Mexico border? My head was spinning, and this just wasn't gonna fly.

No way. No how. I wasn't living apart from my husband.

I now had some seriously serious questions. I hit hard with life-altering questions such as, "Who's gonna scratch my back on any given Tuesday night?" and, "Am I supposed to cook dinner for just me?" and, "What if I have a flat tire and you're all of twelve hours away? Do I just sit and wait for you? Huh? Or do I have to call roadside assistance? I didn't marry roadside assistance, I married you. So, I guess I'll just need to pack a lunch and some books to read every time I get in the car in case I have a flat tire now."

He remained oddly calm. Never flinched. Broke no sweat.

I tell you, the man has the patience of Job.

Yeah, Job. You know that guy in the Bible whose wife encouraged him to give up, curse God, and die? Man, what a keeper she must've been. And I don't know exactly what it was she was all up in arms about because, well, I'm no Bible scholar. But she must've been a real treat to live with. At least I'm not like her. I'm supportive, remember?

I listen. I'm openminded. I don't jump to conclusions.

"I'm just asking that you, for once, be openminded about this and listen. Stop jumping to your made-up conclusions. Please consider the options before you say no. I really think this could be a good thing for us."

A good thing? For us?

How in tarnation was living hours away from each other, not seeing each other every evening, me having to learn to FaceTime, scratching my own back on doorframes, and texting the occasional *how's it going?* nineteen times a day gonna be a good thing for us? I was pretty sure I was a part of this *us* he's referring to, and I could assure you . . . this wouldn't be a good thing for my part of *us*.

Little did I know I had just been handed, quite possibly, one of the best blessings life has ever offered me.

Once he was able to shut me up long enough to listen to the actual details, this didn't seem to be anything like I had convinced myself it was going to be.

No living apart.

No trying to feed this family on my income while keeping my wine cellar stocked up. If you call a bottle or two in the fridge a wine cellar.

No twelve-hour commute.

No scratching my back on doorframes.

No nothing I had myself all riled up over.

Imagine that. I was wrong.

Because it's so hard for me to ever swallow actually being wrong, I still found myself trying to convince myself this was a bad thing. Nothing good could come of living so far away from family. From friends. From the life I had been building in this city for over fifteen years.

What if I didn't like it? But what about the people there? They might hate me. What if I couldn't learn the language? I knew I'd still be in Texas, but it's right on the border, for Heaven's sake! But I might get homesick. What if I couldn't learn how to make homemade tortillas? But it's the desert. I'll be living in the desert. Where it's hot. Unforgivably hot. Hotter than a stolen tamale. What if my lily-white skin just sizzled right off the bone? What if, what if, what if? But . . .

After some long talks with God and soul searching on my part, I finally just looked in the mirror and said those mighty words of wisdom I've said so often to myself just prior to making a change I wasn't too sure about:

If "what ifs" and "buts" were candy and nuts, it'd be Christmas around here all year.

And there you have it. The secret to my decision making is out.

His résumé was prepared. Applications were processed. Appointments were made. Interviews were had. Phone calls were made. More interviews were had. Waiting was done. More waiting was done. An offer was made.

Screeeech.

Put on the brakes right here, big boy.

"They offered you the job? Already? Just where are we supposed to live down there on the border in this little desert town where I hear it's hotter than a toothless hooker on payday? And do they even have a church? Where am I supposed to go to church down there? If there's no church, I ain't going!"

I throw my sainthood around when convenient. And necessary.

Keith was secretly hoping I would have asked about this part much sooner or, at best, I would have forgotten about this part altogether. But no. I asked on the day he was ready to accept the offer on this newfound retirement job.

And honestly, if I would have thought about it sooner, I would have asked. But I never expected to get to this point. I never anticipated this retirement job stuff actually coming full circle anytime in my lifetime.

I'm really good about thinking if I don't acknowledge something, it'll just go away.

Hasn't worked once in my fifty years. At least not yet.

Sure, I had zero doubts about Keith being offered the job. Heck, I had more faith in him than he did. I regularly preached left and right to him with, "If this is where God wants you to be, He'll make a path," and, "God has the last say-so in everything," and, "Just pray, then leave it up to God to guide us where to go from here."

I was just your modern-day Tammy Faye Baker. Less the smudgy, black tears.

Plus, those churched-up words were spewed simply to buy me some time on all of this. I was pretty sure God wanted me to stay right where I was, doing just what I was doing. He didn't want me going anywhere. Not now, anyway. I was sure of it.

And another thing that was going to prolong this little event in our life? The great state of Texas. Everybody knows any state agency moves a tad slower than a snail's pace. On anything and everything it does. Or doesn't do. The state is never in a hurry. The state is never speedy. The state is never concerned about missing a deadline. If you tell the state to hurry up, it'll just look at you and shrug. The state does not care.

If you're gonna do business of any kind with a state agency, you better get ready to hurry up and wait. And bring a snack. Or three.

I really felt I had plenty of time to kill. I figured he'd get some sort of offer he couldn't make heads or tails of in about three years. I could worry about living arrangements and sweaty armpits then. Figured I had plenty of time. But again, no. Three short months after he clicked "send" on that email with his attached résumé . . . it was done. Before I realized it, he was ready to load up a U-Haul truck.

But just where did he think he was going to unload that U-Haul truck?

"Well, they've offered me three months to get moved. We can get the house on the market, start packing, and be there in no time. And it's perfect timing. Cayla is off at college, so we really have no reason to hang around here. Unless you want to keep griping about getting up at the butt crack of dawn and sitting in traffic for over an hour. Your words, not mine. Then sitting in a cube under fake lighting for another eight hours. Again, your words, not mine. If that's really what you want, we'll just stay right here and keep doing the same ol' thing."

And just like that, this was all finally becoming real. In my face kind of real. This was now becoming something I couldn't run from, like a crying baby or a hotel bill.

And it's not that I didn't maybe want this change. I just wasn't sure I was ready for such a change. But whoever really is? I mean, I was comfortable. I liked where we were in life. Everything was calm and serene. Everything fit, like an old comfortable pair of dirty sneakers.

But if I'm honest, it was becoming a bit humdrum. Same commute. Same job. Same grocery store. Same restaurants. Same this. Same that. It was starting to feel as if we were outgrowing this life. Like, there was something more out there, but we didn't know what. So, though I would have cut my tongue out before admitting I was secretly excited about this change, I'll admit to you, I was kinda excited about this change. I figured I could jump, and the good Lord would catch me like he's done so many times before, or I could jump and learn to fly.

At that time, I didn't realize it, but I was fighting to let go of, well, I didn't really know what. A mundane existence? A life where boredom was making a home? The "same ol' thing?" Though things often seemed messy and a bit out of my control, I was learning how to not fear the fear of not knowing. I was seeing I needed to accept the change that could possibly bring endless excitement. I was making myself acknowledge my uncertainty.

This path I wasn't sure of getting on? It was my path. It was designed for me. And I could either get on that path and experience all the joy and happiness and excitement it was holding, or I could sit on the sideline and wonder if this was all there was to life.

But Keith did not need to know any of this just yet. For I was ready . . . I just hadn't accepted the fact that I was ready.

Little did I know I had just been handed, quite possibly, one of the best blessings life has ever offered me.

Between you and me, I kinda had secret hopes the house would take forever to sell. I mean, it wasn't my fault if the house didn't sell and there's no one who wanted to buy it and it just sat there and sat there and sat there. That would buy me some time without it being my fault.

The very first day it was listed? Sold.

You heard me.

First day. Sold.

Most folks would have immediately shouted, "Thank you, Jesus!" with hands raised high to the heavens, but no . . . not me. I shouted, "Jesus, are you kidding me?!?" with my hands planted firmly on my hips.

I remember being a bit annoyed when the realtor called early that first morning it was on the market. A Saturday morning. My Saturday morning. Only one of the two days in seven I didn't have to actually wake up before the sun, fake a smile, and try my best to be charming. He wanted to schedule a showing. In not so many words, what I heard was, "What's the soonest you can disappear so I can attempt to make a hefty commission on your house, sweetie?"

I didn't even get dressed. Just threw on some lipstick, fluffed the bedhead out, slipped on my flip flops, and put the car in reverse. All while still not wearing a bra and still in the pajamas I slept in. That's just how much excitement exuded through my veins. I slowly pulled out of the driveway about four minutes before they were to show up. I leisurely drove through the neighborhood, hoping to not see any neighbors. I mean, surely this couldn't take more than eight minutes. It's a house. It's got a roof. Nice yard. Pool. Decent landscaping. Just a house. Our house. But just a house.

To keep that nice man mowing his yard a street over—who I passed and waved at no less than seven times—from thinking I was casing the joint, I decided to just stop the car and wait. I sat in my car, two driveways down from ours, in the blazing heat of the Texas summer sun, for no less than forty-five minutes. Parked just where I could see what was going on at our house, but far enough out of range for them to see me. Snooping. Nosing. Investigating. Busybodying. Whatever you want to call it. But mostly waiting. And watching for them to leave so I could get back to my Saturday morning of doing a bunch of nothing.

They were there long enough to call for squatters' rights. I expected to see them fire up the grill in the backyard. Splash in the pool. Water the plants.

After what felt like an eternity of sitting in my car just down the street, I watched them slowly pull out of our driveway. As they made their left turn out of the neighborhood, I drove back in my driveway, pulled into my garage, trekked into my house.

When I say my phone rang less than twelve minutes later, I mean my phone rang less than twelve minutes later. It was Keith. The realtor had already called him with news of an offer. These early morning lookers made an offer. And get this: of a bit more than asking price.

Though I've never understood it, how is that an offer? An offer is when you want to buy something for less than what they want to sell it for, right? So I guess they basically said, "We're going to buy your house. Pack up and get out. Now."

"What? Who buys a house with no negotiating? That's crazy talk. They're not serious. And this is stupid. It's been on the market one day. Nobody buys a house the first day it's on the market without making any kind of negotiations. And anybody with half the sense God gave a goose doesn't offer more than what the asking price is. Have you ever heard me say, *Allow me to purchase these $25 heels for $100?* No. No, you haven't. That's stupid. And we're not selling to stupid people. Are leftovers okay for supper tonight?"

Not only did they buy our house for above asking price, but they also threw in extra for my washer and dryer. As well as his lawnmower and weed eater.

Later that evening when Keith came home from work, I'm sure you can imagine the preaching-to I got.

"Well, you were right! You said God has the last say-so in everything and that He'll guide us where to go from here. This must be a sign from above! I got the job, and the house sold. This is all working together like a well-oiled machine! Just like you said!"

My very own words. Used against me. What nerve.

We closed on the house and handed over the keys just a short three stupid weeks later.

Little did I know I had just been handed, quite possibly, one of the best blessings life has ever offered me.

Before I knew it, I turned in my resignation while refusing any sort of *later on, loser, and get out of here* party from my coworkers, we placed our whole life in storage, and we packed up our RV with a few weeks' worth of clothes and my Bible. Yes, my Bible. I mean, I figured if Jesus got me into this mess, I might as well make him come along with us. We decided to take those next couple of months and travel. Relax. Rest. Embrace my fear. Embrace my uncertainty.

Our first stop? Big Bend Ranch State Park.

We headed west and drove. For hours.

It was on that trip I faced the fact that the state of Texas isn't big. It's unfathomably huge. Stupidly large. Giant.

It's been said that Texas is the most recognizable state in the world. I don't rightly know who said it, but it's been said. Trust me. It's big. And I can vouch for that. It's just a mere eight hundred and one miles north to south and a brief seven hundred seventy-three miles east to west.

To put that into perspective, Houston to Dallas is about the same distance as Paris to London. And that big gap from Houston to New York City? It's about the same as that big gap from Houston to Los Angeles.

And those are all places I ain't praying to live. Paris? London? NYC and LA? I'm sure they're nice enough and all. I just don't wanna call 'em home.

One reason is that we have something they all don't have.

Pecan pie.

And that's pronounced *puh-cahn*. Not *pee-can*. Emphasis on the "cahn."

Anyway, we drove for hours. Hours, I tell you. As part of an incentive with this new job thing, Keith was told we could live on state property. There were three residences available for us to choose from. I've never had an employer offer to let me live in the parking garage, much less on the property of my office. Just how sweet of the state to offer this! Odd, but sweet. Thanks, but no thanks. I was quite sure we could find something on our own.

Wrong. They weren't being sweet at all with that so-called incentive. They were being all *live on property or live in a tent* was what they were being. The closest town was small. Meaning, a gas station, a super small market, and maybe three people. Two being gas station clerks. With the other running the super small market.

The first two options were a no.

I do believe when I saw the first option, I said, "No. The shed you kept your lawnmower in back home was bigger than this. I can't even turn around in it without bumping into you. No."

Then after seeing the second option, I barked out, "It's all but sitting in the middle of the highway. Hello, road noise, thank you for not letting me sleep! And what's with all this big equipment and these tractor-looking things parked all around it? This is a maintenance barn, isn't it? The state is offering us a maintenance barn for a house? This ain't gonna fly. Get me the number to the governor . . . "

Keith's hopes were dwindling and dwindling fast. There was one so-called option left. And my attitude had pretty much already decided where the state could put any and every option it offered.

We turned off the main highway and drove fifteen miles over a gravel road. I rolled up my window because of the dust. It was sticking to my lip gloss and making my lips gritty. We made a left turn down, well, another gravel road and drove another three miles. Up a hill, around the bend, past some deserted horse stables. Nothing but mountains and valleys all around me. No signs of life, except for cacti, which I think should be called cactuses . . . but that's another story. And other stuff with thorns and quills on it. And that big, nasty-looking hairy pig thing I saw scampering through the brush. Which, I was informed, was a javelina. Which is not a pig but a rodent.

Well, glory be. As if a rodent was so much more welcome in my life than a pig. Pfft.

As we topped the last hill, I saw it.

The most perfect little cottage nestled deep in this valley of hills. For a minute, I thought I spotted Julie Andrews turning in circles singing "The Hills are Alive."

I assumed this was some sort of rental cottage or maybe an information center for the park. But it certainly could not be our third option. No way, no how. I ain't living that good.

But no. This was option number three. Our last option. Our final option. Our "take it or leave it and go home" option.

And I immediately loved it.

As we pulled up to this quaint little homestead, I asked a few questions:

"What are those big panel-looking things on the side of the house?"

Solar panels. Because I didn't see any electrical lines.

"What about that little shed in the back fenced area? What's in there?"

Propane generator. For if solar energy runs out of the panels, I could still have generated power.

"And that big concrete tub? The one stuck out there in those old horse pens?"

Water cistern. Because I liked to have water when I bathed.

It was like I was Annie Oakley living on some old Wild West movie set. While it had a lot of nothing, it somehow had everything.

It was the most beautiful piece of land I'd ever gawked at, though it was quite primitive and secluded. Smack in the middle of three hundred thirty thousand state-owned acres that we wouldn't have to mow. My nearest neighbors were seventeen miles away. Therefore, because of that reason alone, they immediately became my dearest neighbors.

We stepped onto the front porch and peered through the windows. Wooden floors and wooden ceilings. Thick adobe walls. Fresh paint. An old clawfoot bathtub, original to the house. And yet . . . a modern, updated kitchen. While the adobe exterior was kept intact, the interior had been completely updated. But updated to its original time period. Which I later discovered was around the late 1800s.

I looked around the area. At the mountains, the mesas, the creek bed. I heard nothing. Well, nothing except for a light breeze. And a few cooing doves.

However, no school buses. No sirens. No neighbors' dogs barking. The only movement, besides the breeze rustling through the one lone tree in the yard, was a couple of jackrabbits scampering through the briar jungle just over yonder. Everything about this place was moving at its own pace. Which appeared to be slower than molasses running uphill.

I wasn't sure I had ever witnessed such true peace and quiet before. Heck, I wasn't sure I even knew what true peace and quiet were until that very moment.

But somehow, it's like I could feel my soul slowing down. My spirit relaxing. Every muscle fiber unwinding. If that's even possible for me.

"This is it."

Keith then started asking some questions I never even let penetrate my ear holes. I held my hand up and just shook my head.

"This is it. It's like when I first met you, I just knew. I don't know how or why I knew, but I just knew. And I have that same feeling now. This is it. Let's do it."

Little did I know, I had just been handed, quite possibly, one of the best blessings life has ever offered me.

Arrangements were made with the sweet Lone Star State, and this would be our new home. Within a week of peering through those windows, I found myself driving a trailer with most of our belongings in it while following Keith in our RV with all the rest. It felt strange. None of those belongings included skirts and heels. None of those belongings included heavy traffic and a slow commute. And none of those belongings included a mundane existence and boredom.

For I had left all of that behind.

My dad always preached to us kids, "Life ain't no dress rehearsal." And he's right. It's not. You get one shot and one shot only. Once the curtain is up, you gotta perform. Make it a great performance. Don't sit in the corner. Don't stand frozen in fear. Don't wait for applause. Look at the world square in the face and dance. Dance your dance. Be center stage with bells on.

Keep in mind, there will be some of that corny, dramatic movie music that reminds you fear, and uncertainty is just around the corner. Or a shark fin just over the waves. But just how good is any memorable performance without a little fear? A little uneasiness? A little doubt?

Remember, fortune favors the brave. Be adventurous enough to shoot embarrassingly high. Have more guts in life than you can hang on a fence.

Why?

Because having more guts in life than you can hang on a fence can bring you many of life's greatest blessings.

That's why.

My first year living in that little cottage in the desert? I can easily say that was, so far, the best year of my life. Things moved much slower, and living without a few modern conveniences taught me how to make do and do without.

Who needs a dryer in your washroom when you have a perfectly good clothesline and pins? Who needs a treadmill in a gym when you have a twisting, winding gravel road? Who needs skylights in their living room when you have open skies holding more bright and twinkling stars than you could ever count each night? And who needs a pew in a church when you have God whispering directly to your heart amongst your very own mountains and valleys with every grateful prayer you weep?

Always know, God will not ask you to do anything He hasn't already paved the path for. The path He's already walked for you. The path He's ready to now walk with you. Even if that path is paved in gravel and dirt. It's your path He has designed just for you.

You can either get on that path and experience all the joy and happiness and excitement He's offering or you can sit on the sideline and wonder, *Is this all there is to life?*

I pray when you find yourself contemplating making a good, positive change in life and in your soul, you hear God whisper, "I need to talk to you about something," then you'll do yourself a favor. Trust Him. Just try it. Listen to your heart. Listen to your faith. Listen to your soul.

But just don't pass it up. Don't pass up the joy. The happiness. The excitement. Because all of these things have been designed just for you.

By Him.

For at that very moment you may have just been handed, quite possibly, one of the best blessings life has ever offered you.

PSALM 107:9

For He satisfies the longing soul,
and the hungry soul He fills with good things.

• CHAPTER 6 •

YOUR DUCKS WILL NEVER BE ALL IN A ROW, SO JUST QUIT WRANGLIN' 'EM AND LET 'EM FLY.

As I've matured, I've found myself becoming more ladylike. And we both know that is nothing more than my churched-up version of *as I've aged*.

I'll never understand why, oh why, I insist on being uncomfortable and fighting what I feel is right.

It's like it's a cardinal sin and I'm determined to doom myself to an existence of constant eye rolling.

"They are way too high, my toes are blue and numb, but these heels look fabulous!" Rather than maybe wait for my size to hit the inventory. But no, I buy them anyway.

"It's a little too snug, I have to safety pin the zipper together to keep it from blowing apart, and I probably shouldn't try to sit down in it, but this skirt is to die for!" Rather than maybe accept the fact my curves are a little too much for this old thing and buy a new one. But no, I wear it anyway.

"There are way more calories than the heavens should allow in this stuff, I'm gonna put myself into a diabetic coma with all that sugary sweetness, but I'm doing this dessert!" Rather than maybe stick with eating healthy and doing what I know is best for my well-being. But no, I eat it anyway.

82

I have no shame.

When things are too tight, too irritating, too uncomfortable, do you think maybe that's a sign it's a good time for a good change?

Me, neither.

I usually just keep limping along, sucking it in, and blaming life for simply being life. Just as stubborn as a blind mule.

Thanks to some struggles life has thrown my way, a few mistakes, and more *what in tarnation was I thinking* times than I care to admit to, I've grown to realize coming into my calling means coming out of my comfort zone.

Let's face it. None of us enjoy making those big, life-changing decisions. And if you're like me, you'll avoid making them for as long as possible. Just lay low and don't make eye contact, which is what I always say.

So, you ask, "But what if he turns out to be a big loser and not be *the one* for me after all?"

But what if he is *the one* and you can't imagine life without him?

Then you worry, "But what if I take the job, I hate it, then I'm stuck?"

But what if you love it and it takes you to new places?

Next you fear, "But what if he changes and promises to never cheat again?"

But what if he doesn't and you've wasted all those years not being loved the way you deserve?

You see, these questions? You've probably asked yourself questions similar to these at one time or another. But for me? These are some of the very questions I've asked myself at different points in my life. I can waste so much time what-iffing life better than anyone I know. Back and forth and back and forth. I can wear myself down to the bone in no time flat. Believe it or not, I can be simply impossible at times.

When Keith and I decided to . . . wait a minute. Let's keep it real. There was no "Keith and I" deciding anything. It was me. It was all me doing the deciding on our little retirement move to this small border town. No way no how was he going to prove to me marriage could be heaven, then sell the house, leave his career of over twenty-five years, and make all these changes to our life without my blessing.

When the queen is happy, there is peace in the kingdom.

And this queen better be happy for the sake of his kingdom.

I was the judge and the jury on this little life or death case.

So allow me to start over.

When *I* decided we should sell the house, I should leave my job, and we should make the life changes necessary for him to semi-retire and move out to the other side of nowhere, I found myself getting a tad uncomfortable.

Okay. If it's just us talking, we're gonna keep it real. I didn't get a tad uncomfortable; I got all kinds of uncomfortable. Things were too tight. Too irritating. Too stressful.

Now, let's say we make this big life-changing move and we're living over yonder being all desert-y and hot and sweaty on the border where it gets hotter than a billy goat's butt in the pepper patch. What was I supposed to do to keep myself busy during the day? I shouldn't have to find another job because he wants a retirement job! Who was I going to bother? I didn't know anybody there and I wasn't in the mood to make friends! How was I going to keep my mind from going to mush? What would I do without a bunch of traffic? Just what was I gonna eat? Okay, that eating part really wasn't that big of a deal, but there were all kinds of questions popping up that I had no answers for. And the worst part? I wouldn't have any answers to any questions until I got there.

Which led me to a whole other group of concerns. Like, what if I hated it there? What if nobody liked me? What if I got homesick and just couldn't do it? What if I couldn't learn Spanish? What if I couldn't make tortillas?

I just knew I was gonna be as lonely as a pine tree in a parking lot living down there.

I was getting really nervous and really unsure about coming out of this comfort zone thing of mine. I mean, it's called my comfort zone for a reason, for Heaven's sake. Because that's where I'm the most comfortable. Duh. So why in tarnation would I ever choose to leave where I'm the most comfortable?

I might not love the long commutes and traffic, but I was comfortable with it. I might not love the mundane existence where boredom was making a home, but I was all right with it. I might not love tight skirts and heels, but I tolerated them. And looked absolutely stunning while doing it, I might add.

Okay, maybe I did or maybe I didn't. But if you don't think you're quite stunning, no one is going to think you're quite stunning. And a southern woman must always feel she's the sparkling diamond in a rhinestone world. Even if there are days she's the only one telling herself that. And there will be those days. Trust me.

Anyway, all those irritating and stressful things? It's what I knew. It's what I was used to. It's what I was good at. And as ridiculous as it sounds, when it's what you know, when it's what you're used to, and when it's what you're good at? Then let me be the one to tell you, it's what you're comfortable with. I mean, if you acknowledge all that discomfort and those irritations, you're then gonna have to do something about them. And who has time for that?

Finally, after a long chat session with God, with me doing most of the chatting, of course, it hit me like a ton of bricks. The absolute worst thing that could happen was we could hate it and just make another change. Period.

And between me and you, no matter how much I was fighting it, I really felt this was the path He had laid out for me. It was even kind of exciting in a secretive *don't tell anyone because I'm not eating any crow* kind of way. But knowing that didn't ease my nerves much at all. However, if you sit quiet and shut up for a while, you'll see that God whispers. And in my heart, all I could hear was Him whispering:

"You'll either learn to fly or I will catch you. Just be bold."

Still, though. My nerves were trying to get the best of me. I had to keep telling myself I wasn't going to develop some incurable itch from a heat rash. And I certainly wasn't going to find myself playing in a mariachi band. We were just making a change. A simple move. People do it every day. No big deal.

It's just that this change was hours away from civilization, mind you. To the desert. On the border. But it was just a simple little move. It's certainly not the worst thing that could happen.

No, actually sometimes the worst thing that can happen is people. People and their opinions. And their fears. And their inconveniences. And all their questions they like to dump on you because they don't have answers. And now, not only do you have your own fears and concerns . . . you have theirs, too.

The folks weren't crazy about us making this move. Your typical worrisome *you're going to die down there then I'm gonna say I told you so* parents: "Do you have any idea how dangerous it is on the border? Dope smugglin' and cartel killins' and, well, just all kinds of things! Don't you ever watch the news? Young lady, you better straighten up before I yank a knot in your tail. Act like you got some sense!"

And Cayla was totally inconvenienced. Your typical, over-dramatic *it's all about me and what makes me happy* college teenager: "Where am I supposed to go for holidays now? I'm not driving down there. What are my friends going to say? Why can't you just buy a house in the city and pay a huge mortgage every month so I can come home twice a year? This isn't what you're supposed to do! You're supposed to live your life by making my life easy!"

And friends were simply at a loss. Your typical inquisitive *so you're not gonna be keeping up with the Joneses anymore* confidants: "The border? That's, like, hundreds of hours away. Will we ever see you again? How big is the house? Does it have a pool? Why would you do this? Is there even a country club in the area? Do they have wineries down there?"

You see? Not everyone is going to be your cheerleader.

It was starting to occur to me: *When God whispers yes, it doesn't matter who screams no.*

I've found that sometimes, when you walk your own path in life, no matter how happy you want everyone to be, it may not sit well with others. Why? Because it doesn't work for them. It doesn't fit 'em just right. But always remember that's their problem and not yours. You can either live your life for you or you can live your life for them. That's your choice. Either way, at the end of the day, you're the one stuck with the outcome. And remember what I told you my dad always preached to us girls growing up? Life ain't no dress rehearsal. There are no do overs.

And okay, maybe I exaggerated a tad bit on everyone's comments just now, but you get the drift. Very few were genuinely happy about this decision being made. This decision was made by us and for us. It made them uncomfortable. They might have to worry about us. They might have to drive a little farther. We might not be around for every happy hour. And I know darn good and well their fears and concerns were all out of love, but again . . . we could live our life for them or we could live our life for us.

And I also know beyond a shadow of a doubt they all were certain we didn't have the sense God gave a goose. They just couldn't bring themselves to say it.

But really? Isn't that what we all do? Want others to live a life or do things that make our lives a little easier? Make us feel a little better about things? Maybe take our feelings into consideration when they're making decisions for them?

Like how you wish your girlfriend would just shut her pie hole about how great her new guy is. Why? Maybe because you can't get a call back after a first date. Or how you try your best to convince your kid the local college is best, but they really like the one in another state. Why? Maybe because you really aren't emotionally ready for them to move too far away just yet. Oh, and what about that time you didn't answer the phone because you just couldn't take another hour of her yammering about that great, most perfect ever job she landed . . . over six months ago? Why? Maybe because you're still stuck at that same old dead-end job for what seems like an eternity now and you know you're going nowhere.

No matter what or who it's about . . . I think it's natural that we want them to make it easy and convenient for us.

As silly as it sounds, I do it. I'm ashamed to admit I'm quite guilty of doing that very thing. I want it to be easy and convenient for me, even if it's all about you.

And honestly, not only family and friends thought we had gone off the deep end. I, too, was starting to worry about my sanity. My anxiety was lying to me about something it knew nothing about regarding this move and getting me all riled up. Just completely flustered. A bunch of crazy talk that made no sense to nobody but there I was, just a-listening anyway. I don't get me, either, sometimes.

Anxiety. There's a friend who comes around too often. Uninvited and full of advice. The advice you didn't ask for. The advice you don't need. The advice that isn't even useful. But we sit a spell and visit with her anyway. Offer her a chair on the front porch. A nice afternoon tea. Why, it'd be just downright rude not to. Sometimes, we let her eat up our whole day. Or week.

Why do we let our worries and anxiety take over, anyway? Why? Because we know we are always one decision away from a totally different world we're creating for ourselves. So we better decide well.

And isn't it somewhat true we know what we want to do, yet we still want everyone's blessings on things? We starve for that approval . . . that acceptance . . . that membership to the club. That's why we women are known for asking such silliness as, "What would you do if it were you?" when you already know what you should do. And, "Tell me, does that make any sense to you?" when you already know darn good and well it doesn't. And the very one you'll probably never admit to asking but you know you do even if it's just you asking yourself while staring in that full-length mirror, "Does this make me look fat?" when, well . . . you see what I'm saying.

And really, the one question we should all be so much better at asking is, "Who cares?"

Please don't think for one minute I don't care or I'm not concerned about the feelings of others, the very ones who love me the most. No, that's not it at all. But nowhere in my Bible have I found where it says I must please everyone. Or I must make everyone happy with my decisions. Or that I must ask others for their opinions on my arrangements. Especially if the outcome doesn't hold them responsible. And believe me when I tell you I've looked. I've looked high and low, and I can't find it in any book in my Bible.

But I have found where it commands us to love one another.

Dang it.

However, though we may love our family and friends, and we simply want to make those in our life fat and happy as best we can, we must never confuse the command to love with the disease to please. Never. Because if we do, things can get really ugly, real fast for us on the inside. In our thinking. In our decision making. In our heart. And that ain't good for anybody.

While doing all this over-thinking and what-iffing, I had to remind myself of just who I was and whose I was. I was a girl who never liked to follow the crowd, and I liked a good adventure. I tended to live a bit closer to the edge than most. I was a girl who usually always listened for God's whispers when I have big questions in life. I've waited for either that confidence to forge ahead or the uneasiness to steer away. And goodness knows, He has never failed me before. So, if I get the feeling He's behind all this and to forge ahead . . . why am I fighting it so hard? Maybe because it's making me uncomfortable?

Now, there are things in my life I probably should have fought off a little tougher than I did. And I should have waited a bit longer and listened a bit harder for that whisper to come along. I'm pretty sure God wasn't too tickled about a few of those fashion statements I made back in high school, that hideous first marriage, and other things that I jumped on and ran with without waiting on His whispers.

Like that haircut I saw in a magazine and just had to have. Which is one reason why my momma screamed, "For the love of God, what are the neighbors gonna think? Child, you've done gone off the deep end!" when I was sixteen and cut my hair so super short on one side it was basically shaved. Never mind I was being stylish and rocking a hideous punk rock 'do from 1986 that only I could pull off. She was more concerned about the neighbors.

And then there was that time I decided I needed to do something different. Something exciting. I wanted to wear a cute little uniform. And greet passengers with a smile. And point to the over-wing exits that can be found, well . . . over the wings. So I promptly applied with a major airline. For a flight attendant position. And the rest is history. Which is why my momma screamed, "You're moving to where? New York City? For the love of God, what are the neighbors gonna think? You must've done gone and lost your ever lovin' mind!" There we go with those neighbors again.

Down here in the South, we care about what the neighbors think. And I don't rightly know why. I mean, I can explain it to you, but I sure can't understand it for you.

And fear not. I transferred back to an airport on southern soil in no time flat. A southern girl can last for just so long in the north. I mean, there's all that snow. And I couldn't find not one hush puppy on any menu. And you call that sweet tea? Please. Then I found myself constantly answering those same absurd questions of, "Why do you add extra syllables to all your words?" and, "Do you know JR Ewing?" and, "Do you wear cowboy boots?" And then my very favorite of all time: "Is your hair supposed to be that big on purpose?" All that mess right there can just run a poor southern girl ragged.

Anyway. Now finding myself at a new crossroad in life, no matter how hard I tried to fight it, I could hear in my heart God whispering, "You'll either learn to fly or I will catch you. Just be bold."

Before I knew it, Keith and I were loading up a U-Haul with everything we didn't purge when our house sold. And for goodness sake, did that feel good. Life should be purged more often than we do it, don't you think? Getting rid of stuff you don't need and things that don't make you happy and don't bring out your absolute best is at the top of my list. From pots and pans to shoes to people to opinions. Purge it, sister.

As nervous as I was about all this, as unsure as I was if this was really my path to be on, as much as I questioned my sanity, nobody ever said you can't be bold and afraid at the same time. I mean for goodness' sake.

Plus, your ducks will never be all in a row, so you might as well quit wranglin' 'em and just let 'em fly.

So, before I knew it, there I was on this big interstate. Driving his *too big for me to drive but I'm driving it anyway* truck with a trailer attached. And let me tell you, it felt like I was driving that thing for days. That trailer held all of our furniture and big stuff on it. Yes, we had purged our life down to a trailer of furniture. And stuff. And he drove the RV while pulling my *just the right size for me to drive* Jeep. With clothes and other stuff packed securely in the RV. We were on our way.

To our new home. To our new life. To our new adventure.

We drove. And drove. And drove some more. Separate. Alone. Apart. Me in the truck and him not. This meant I had no one to panic to when my ridiculous thoughts overtook my brain that was already bogged down with all my over-thinking. I only had me to talk to, and that ain't good for anyone. Especially me.

We were getting closer to our new life, and I was getting even more uncomfortable than before we left. And by then, I should have realized something. Just like all those fabulous pairs of heels I just couldn't pass up whether they were on sale or not, before anything new fits just right, it's bound to be a bit uncomfortable. At least until you get used to it and put some wear on it.

Eventually, we made it. To our new home. Our new life. Our new adventure or whatever this was going to be. And as soon as I topped the hill and once again saw that little cottage, something came over me. Something calming. Something peaceful. Something quiet. I began to feel that this change was really going to be okay. *I was going to be okay.*

And for the first time, I heard myself whisper, *I will either learn to fly or He will catch me. But regardless, I will be bold.*

There may or may not have been a weepy moment that occurred right there coming over that hill that I've kept between me and God. Until now, anyway.

Like I said earlier, we had whittled life down quite a bit. So, since we didn't bring much, we didn't unpack much. This house was much smaller than the house we came out of, so already life was seeming a whole lot simpler. Less sweeping, less dusting, less fussing. Less everything, it seemed.

After the dizziness of getting things in order, pictures hung, and me arguing basically with just me because he really didn't care whether the TV should be against that wall or that wall, life was starting to fit again. It was even starting to feel like a good fit. I was beginning to feel like I had jumped the hurdle that seemed far too high for me to ever clear without falling on my face.

But whether I cleared that hurdle or not, we were here. No more city life. No more traffic. No more high heels.

As Keith's life started its new adventure with his new job, I knew mine had to start, as well.

So, after a morning or two of getting life in order, I went to where I always seem to find myself. To where I can always find some comfort. I needed to feel some normalcy and to discover some familiarity.

Therefore, to the local market I went.

Back home, I knew my market aisle by aisle. I really didn't even need to follow a list, for I was that familiar with the layout. If I started pushing my buggy down the aisles starting from right to left as I entered, I'd begin with fruit on the first aisle and finish up with wine on the last. Which sometimes, depending on my mood and the kind of day I had, was really the only two aisles that mattered.

And yes. You heard that right. Down here in the South, it's a buggy. No baskets for us. Buggies.

But now? I had a new layout to learn. A new path to follow. A new list to make.

Here at the market and in life.

I immediately noticed that this market was much smaller than what I was used to back in the city. But then this town was much smaller than what I was used to back in the city, too.

You'll either learn to fly or I will catch you. Just be bold.

So there I was. At the market. One row of parking that might hold thirty cars on a good day. As opposed to a fully paved parking lot with painted directional arrows, curbside service, and clearly marked parking spaces any Southern Baptist church would be ridiculously envious of. At most, this market held ten regular-sized aisles of canned goods, bread, soft drinks, and a meat/cheese/produce section. As opposed to fifteen double aisles which, if my math serves me well, equals thirty full aisles so long I'd sometimes need a manicure after the time it took to get from one end to the other. Not including the bakery, the expansive produce and fruit sections, and the florist area with beautiful blooming plants and flowers.

None of which this market had.

Actually, it didn't seem to have much at all. Or at least the "much" I was used to sorting and picking through to fill my buggy.

But I guess what my granny used to yell back to me from her sewing room as I was digging through her pantry calling out for where she kept the chocolate MoonPies was true: "If we ain't got it, you don't need it! Plus, you're looking fat lately, anyways!"

Granny . . . bless her heart. I just asked where the MoonPies were, not for any self-confidence killers.

Anyway.

What used to be at least an hour at the market in the city was whittled down to about twenty-two minutes now. And that was if I took my time. I had perused all ten aisles in that short amount of time. Some twice. My buggy held enough, though, to keep me out of the Ten Items or Less aisle and to keep homecooked meals on our table for about three days.

And before you say it, I know it should be *Ten Items or Fewer,* but we don't seem to do things as grammatically correct in the South as the rest of y'all do. I mean, come on. We refer to "dinner" as "supper," and every beverage, except for sweet tea, is called a "Coke." And we fry up everything. Like frog legs, chicken legs, oysters, and on occasion Oreos. Our grammatically challenged wording is certainly not our greatest flaws to the rest of the world.

As I was waiting in the check out line, I stood there smiling and noticed the cashier would not look at me. No eye contact at all. Neither would the gentleman bagging my items. Never had I ever felt more of an outsider than now.

"Excuse me, but may I buy you a water or a Coke?"

They both immediately looked at me. And then they both immediately looked at each other. It was as if life was now in slow motion. But I figured if this was going to be my new market and these were faces I would see on a regular basis, I just might have to take the first step.

Again, out of my comfort zone.

Gustavo, the older gentleman bagging my groceries, smiled at me then said something to Yadira, the cashier. In Spanish.

And in my mind echoed the words, *Oh, sweet heavens, they don't understand me. I don't know Spanish, and they don't know English! What was I thinking? What a fool! I'm now just that crazy redheaded lady who talks to strangers and small children in a language they don't speak! They're gonna run me out of town!*

Then in my heart came the words:

You'll either learn to fly or I will catch you. Just be bold.

I took a deep breath to calm those ever-so-pesty nerves of mine. Reminded myself they're just people and a smile can somehow break any barriers foreign languages may bring.

Yadira smiled and very slowly, while seemingly unsure of her words, replied, "*Gracias*, miss. That is very kind."

I placed two bottles of water on the conveyor belt, pointed to both of them then to the waters. They shook their heads, smiled, and spewed something out in a language I had no clue of. But a smile is always a good sign.

Gustavo buggied my groceries out to my Jeep for me. I was afraid to say anything for fear of no communication. But you know me.

"Do you speak any English?"

"*Pequeno*, English."

And by his smile and small hand gesture, I just knew this meant "not very much."

I did my best with a little small talk as together we unloaded my grocery bags into the Jeep. Somehow, I managed to tell him we just moved to the area and I knew *pequeno* Spanish. He laughed a very hearty laugh and said, "Welcome, lady. *Bienvenido.*"

I smiled and replied with a southern and way too many syllables, "*Gracias, señor!*"

He chuckled and encouraged me with, "Very, very good!" in his broken English. My smile must've had told him I would be seeing him regularly. For it was then he said, "I teach you Spanish and you teach me more English."

I laughed with a nod and shook his hand.

After two weeks, my visits to the market with my awkward attempts at Spanish with Yadira and Gustavo began forming unlikely friendships.

"Hello" became "*hola.*" "Water" became "*agua.*" "Thank you" became "*gracias.*" "How are you?" became "*Como estas?*"

What once was a handshake was now a hug.

And what were once unsure strangers had unknowingly become faithful friends.

The Christmas holiday was now upon us. That large bottle of vanilla from Gustavo's home country just over the border was absolutely splendid. As were Yadira's homemade Mexican cinnamon cookies, a recipe passed through her family over the years. They both were so appreciative of the festively wrapped plates of fudge I graciously handed them.

But the best gift I received was a hug from each. With a joyful "*Feliz Navidad*" attached.

Then Gustavo called me family.

What a gift in itself.

Keith's work schedule allowed him to be off for Christmas Day. Though we were new to the area and less than a month or so old there, we both felt we needed to spend that morning somewhere we always find some comfort. We needed to feel some normalcy and to discover some familiarity.

Therefore, to the local Catholic church we went.

Not that we had many other options. The Hispanic community nurtures a strong Catholic faith. And we were now proud members of a small border town. Plus, you know what they always say, "When in a small border town . . . " I've never figured out just who *they* are.

I was raised in the Catholic church, and though Keith was not, he knew enough to know when to kneel, when to stand, when to kneel, and when to kneel. Then when to kneel again.

As we walked into this old mission church built back in 1683, I felt a calm. I felt a peace. Life felt like it just fit. Not much was uncomfortable anymore. Not much was irritating. Or stressful.

The church was filled to the choir loft with poinsettias, a flawless nativity scene, and families dressed in their absolute best.

We took our seats. Not too close to the front, but not in the back row, either. Just before mass started, a young girl stopped at our row and asked if we would be so kind as to bring the gifts to the altar.

During mass.

Us.

My first instinct was to say, "Thank you, but no. I'm not walking the bread and wine up to the front of this church where I know no one just so I can trip and stumble and probably say a word or two no church ladies should hear on a Christmas morning and end up finding myself banned from here."

However, Keith's first instinct was to say, "We would be honored."

Dang it.

Let me back up a bit so this'll make a little more sense for you.

You see, Keith and I married about two years before making that big move to that small cottage in that border town.

But when we started our life together, we never actually walked down the aisle.

Well, not together, anyway.

We had both done it before, just with the wrong ones.

No, when we married, it was a simple ceremony at our home. No long, white dress. No crowded church pews. No music. No party afterward. Just us, Cayla, and the pastor.

So, even though Keith and I vowed the vows, prayed the prayers, and did the kiss a little over two years prior, I never really felt like an *us* until we made that big move to that small little cottage in that border town.

For some reason, after all the dizziness of getting life in order in our new home in our new adventure, our new life had started to feel like the gift it was.

Just then, it hit me like a ton of bricks:

God had given us these gifts.

This gift of a new home. This gift of a new life. This gift of a new adventure.

And it was now our turn to give Him a gift.

Our gift of gratitude.

You'll either learn to fly or I will catch you. Just be bold.

Neither of us tripped.

I didn't drop the wine.

He didn't fumble the bread.

It wasn't uncomfortable.

We survived.

We both soon realized we had been blessed with a new life that was certainly a new adventure.

And God started it off by walking us down the aisle.

Together.

Toward Him.

On Christmas morning.

So, sweet friend, when you find things feeling a bit uncomfortable and you see you may be fighting what you feel is right and the path you should be on, it may be a gentle reminder that coming into your calling means coming out of your comfort zone.

And if you sit still for a moment and just listen, you may find it to be a soft whisper from God that now is a good time for a good change.

Because regardless, you will either learn to fly or He will catch you. But you must always be bold.

JOSHUA 1:9

Have I not commanded you?
Be strong and courageous.
Do not be frightened, and do not be dismayed,
for the Lord your God is with you wherever you go.

CHAPTER 7

SOMETIMES THE VERY THING THAT SEEMS AS THOUGH IT COULDN'T POSSIBLY BE ENOUGH TURNS OUT TO BE MORE THAN ENOUGH.

"You're positive? You are absolutely, without a doubt, certain there are no gators in this murky water? I know you say you've never seen or heard of any out here, but I really don't think they're too picky about the waters they keep. They've been around for like thirty-seven million years. They're modern-day dinosaurs, you know? I've always just figured 'em to be giant swimming armadillos. Also, you know that death roll thing they do when they're trying to kill you? They can't do it if they can't move their tail. That's why, when you see pictures of one caught in a neighborhood because apparently it thought it needed to go into town for something, there's usually someone sitting on its tail and not just its mouth. Let me tell you one thing, I see a gator out here on this river, Jesus ain't gonna be the only one known for walking on water. I love you and all, but if I see a big lizard face surface this water, you're on your own . . . been nice knowing you."

Apparently, I'd spent a little too much time around the swampy southern bayous and listening to too many tales from the Cajun kinfolk.

Or watching too much Animal Planet.

Though there was not a cypress tree covered in Spanish moss to be found, I was sure I was bound to see two beady eyes rise up through the cloudy waters of the Rio Grande River. Rudely staring. Intimidatingly bubbling. Sinfully smiling. At me.

Keith reassured me he had never heard of alligators making their way from the marshlands of my old neck of the woods back in East Texas to the southern West Texas/Mexico border. And even though I was several feet ahead of him, paddling my own kayak, I could feel him rolling his eyes and slowly shaking his head at the absurdity of my questions and gator facts.

Quite interesting facts, if I say so myself.

And you can un-scrunch your face. The answer is yes.

I do have my very own kayak.

And stop laughing. I know the thought of lip glossing and kayaking don't hardly go together. But believe me, it can be done. I insisted on having my own back when he was looking to purchase his. Well, because I wanted my own. That's why.

The older I get, the more I see life handing me adventures I never even asked for, much less wanted. Especially now that my life is anchored to a small border town, a husband who seeks out adventures, and a terrain any rock-climbing billy goat would be totally envious of. Adventures seem to be lurking around almost every corner these days.

We paddled along, and from ahead, I continued educating him on alligators, how these water shoes hurt my feet and were certain to be the least feminine things I owned, and the nation's economy.

Ehem. That last part may have been a bit of a fib since I really don't even like discussing my own economy.

Anyway.

From the highway known as "River Road" that I'm pretty darn sure is the most beautiful scenic route in Texas, I'd looked in awe during many leisurely drives at the winding river that runs along the mountainous border of Texas and Mexico. That river has been rather rough at times, demanding with heavy rapids rushing and pounding against large boulders in its wake. The large rock formations on the mountainsides, as well as the towering landscape that twists and turns in what seems a different direction with each drive I've made up and down this way, can seem to stare at you with utter disdain.

So I knew quite well from the many miles logged driving River Road just what life appeared to be looking from "outside" the river. Looming bluffs with increasingly steep walls. Mad waters pushing and fighting their way downstream. The occasional gang of runaway rocks racing one another to the foot of the mountains only to see who would make the biggest splash.

Looking at life from "outside" the river reveals how rugged the river can be. But never have I wondered just what life would appear to be looking out from "inside" the river.

Glancing toward the road while paddling my kayak in that very river was actually a much different view. Beautiful, rocky peaks rising from the vast terrain. Pristine grounds home to untouched cliffs. A soothing echo of the waters quietly lapping against the banks. The soft whistling of the wind gently blowing through the brush.

And so, this is what looking at life from "inside" the river is like.

Once I found myself inside the river looking out to a place I considered to be very familiar to me, it now appeared to be nothing like what I previously thought.

This is a lot like life, don't you think?

Albeit, though I was completely aware of my location from the curves and hills of River Road I was paddling alongside of, I somewhat felt lost.

Even though everything was the same, everything seemed different.

It was about that time I heard Keith whisper rather loudly to pretty much no one, "Oh, wow. Would you just look at that?"

In that instance, I immediately sold myself the fact there was a giant dinosaur tail slapping the waters and preparing to death roll my kayak. I pulled my paddle out of the water, tucked it inside my kayak, blue-knuckle gripped the edges, and squealed, "OH, SWEET JESUS . . . WHERE? WHERE IS IT?!?"

And though I might not make it to the church pew every Sunday morning, and I sometimes might say a word or two no southern girl who acts like she's got manners should say, annnnd okay, there may or may not be a little dust on my Bible, I found myself ready to break out in song.

Right there. In my kayak. On the Rio Grande. In the best twang I could muster.

And in that same instance, I quickly started digging in my little waterproof bag of, well, a bunch of nothing that I seem to be able to go nowhere without. I had to find my lip gloss.

Because if I was going to meet Jesus, I was going singing. While wearing the most flawless shiny shade of Buttery Begonia money could buy.

However, just as I was about to break out in my twangy rendition of "Then sings my soul, my Savior God, to Thee," he pointed. And that very moment completely changed my singing soul's direction.

"Look over there. Up on the side of that hill. It's got to be at least forty years old. Wow. Isn't that something? Hey, why is the lip gloss out?"

Up on the side of that hill where he was pointing was a car. A yellow car. The older model car looked very much older than, well, me. And like it had been there, lodged in the rocks and wiry brush on the side of that hill, longer than I had been on this earth singing songs to Jesus.

From the placement, it was apparent the car had missed the curve of the road and simply plummeted over the side. You could easily see it had burned there on the rocks. It appeared to be untouched from the time it landed on the side of that hill. For it was too far from the edge of the highway for any type of emergency help to access, and it was much too far from the edge of the river to reach. Plus, the giant rocks and boulders it was lodged in seemed to serve as its final resting place.

It's much different looking out from the inside than it is looking in from the outside. There had apparently been more happenings seen from the river than I was aware of from the road.

After climbing out of that river and loading up those kayaks, I thought about the yellow car for several days. I thought about the driver. I wondered if there was a passenger. I was curious as to the time of day or night that the curve in the road was missed. I speculated on what the last few seconds were possibly like before leaving the road. I hoped leaving the road wasn't intentional. I wondered how, or if, anyone inside was ever even identified.

But, regardless of what the answers to any of those questions might have been, the one question that kept popping into my thoughts was, *Were they happy with the life they were living?*

Which prompted me to ask me the very same question I've asked me so many times at a myriad of life's intersections:

But are you *happy with the life* you're *living?*

And you can bet your southern pastry puff the answer to that question has fluctuated more than my mood two hours into a low-carb diet.

I can only vouch for myself, but sweet mother of all things deceptive, there have been many times in my life I could have won a Tony award for the Broadway-worthy performance I was clinging to.

Why, when I discovered during my first marriage that swindler I was married to was so crooked if he swallowed a nail he'd spit up a corkscrew, even during the heartache, my sham of a smile still continued to light up every room I entered.

At least that's how I made sure everyone in that room regarded me.

And, after many visits with the best fertility doctors this side of the sun, when it was determined never would I experience waking up during the middle of the night in a cold sweat to announce, *"I think it's time,"* my fraudulent joy preceded me around every corner I turned.

At least that's how I made sure everyone else around that corner regarded me.

Except for my family and a few close friends, during times such as those, the rest of the world was safe to assume I was ridiculously happy with the life I was living.

And to be honest, for the most part, I had even myself convinced I was ridiculously happy. Though I was smothering myself in anger and resentment, and at what I don't know, I continued to convince everyone else I was as happy as a tornado blowing through a trailer park.

Once I got rid of about two hundred fifteen miserable pounds simply by divorcing it, I started to see life should be full of adventure. It hit me smack in the heart one day that for the last several years, I had been living for someone else's dreams in that first marriage . . . not mine.

I spent many years in that marriage hearing myself repeat, *"It doesn't matter . . . whatever you want to do."* And you know what? It did matter. I mattered. I had allowed myself to take the backseat to most everything. I was simply existing. No more, no less. Life was "pretty okay" at best. And that was my own fault. For so much of that marriage, I felt like I was on hold. Just watching life roll by. Quietly waiting for my time to come along. And we all know that wasn't going to happen as long as I continued to sit on the sidelines of life.

Life should be a *mission* . . . not an intermission, don't you think? I certainly couldn't expect to find my happiness by waiting on the bench for someone else's. For one day, I may wake up to find all that time I just knew I had . . . was no more.

And that's when I realized maybe I shouldn't be living on the outside of life looking in but instead trying to live in the inside of life and start looking out.

And as the years have passed, I find myself becoming a little more daring and a little less tolerant of the negative things and unfavorable people who leave me feeling empty. I've discovered I feel my best when I don't always play it safe. When I'm bold. When I live a little on the edge. When I make my own path. When I'm somewhat a rebel. When I find myself doing the unexpected. When I try something new for the first time. When I dare myself to go big or go home.

When I continuously remind myself to make this life a great adventure.

Then go live it.

As silly as it sounds, it took most of my time being single after that first marriage to see who I was versus who I wanted to be. It was during that time I decided I will not finish life hearing myself say, *"I wish I would've . . . "* or, *"Why didn't I . . . ?"* Keeping in good conscience, I'd much rather regret doing too much, overwhelming myself, and living a great adventure rather than regret not doing enough and living a safe, mundane, and simple existence.

Now, going back to that little kayaking adventure. That was maybe my third time to captain my own kayak. Yep, you heard me. I was no professional by a long shot. Heck, I wasn't even good enough to be considered a novice at it. It's something I'd never even considered doing. I saw no need to break a perfectly good French-tipped manicured fingernail over a kayak paddle. So, silly things like kayaking or hiking or, well, quite honestly most anything that might cause an undue sweat never entered my mind.

Until one day, when Keith was moseying around some sporting goods store and facetiously asked, "I think I'm going to buy a kayak. I used to have one years ago, and I really enjoyed it. I don't know why I even got rid of it. But I really think I'd enjoy taking it up again . . . you think you'd want one, too?"

Just clear out of the blue, he tossed that question out there. He actually asked me, with a somewhat straight face, if I wanted my own kayak. Really? Who does that? Ridiculous. Did he even know me? And you and I both know he fully expected me to scrunch my face up, glare at him with a curse-filled, non-verbal reply, and completely reject the thought of me paddling my own kayak.

But before I could curl up my nose and dismiss such an asinine inquiry, I heard myself daintily cough out, "You bet your tookus I do!"

I'm not sure which of us was more shocked. For a brief moment, I froze. Right there in my big, *what in the world did I just say out loud*, bug-eyed tracks on aisle seventeen. Then I looked around to see who might have actually sputtered out such nonsense, but there was no one else within three aisles. Just us. So it had to be me.

The next thing I knew, I was being quite bold and picking out a pretty little pink life vest. And of course, he thought pink was a hideous color for a life vest. Never mind I looked flashier than a rat with dark shades and a gold tooth in it. And because he felt pink wasn't the best color for that, I was going to hold off a bit with my request for pink rope lighting to enhance and decorate the outer edge of my kayak.

Oh, and get this. He also simply insisted I refer to it as my "personal flotation device." But I do think life vest sounds a bit more stylish and fashionable, agree?

I mean, think about it. Could you possibly ever fathom hearing me say, *"My, I must say that is a fantastic personal flotation device you're sporting! Wherever did you find that?!?"* Sweet heavens, no.

So here I am, a bit older than I've ever been before, attempting things I've always felt I was, at any other time in my life, too old to attempt.

It's not just me that has started to question my newfound adventurous sanity. Keith periodically does, too. No surprise there, huh? Like that one morning, while he sipped a cup of coffee and I sipped a cup of sugar and creamer with a splash of coffee tossed in, he made the mistake of asking what I wanted to do that day. I all but threw him into cardiac arrest when, out of the clear blue, I daringly suggested we go for a hike.

"Uh, yeah. Okay. You do realize hiking will cause a sweat. You're aware of that, huh? You said something in our wedding vows about never sweating. You're not going to blame any sweating you might do on me later, are you? Is this some kind of set up? And remember, there are all those cacti and sticky thorny things you refer to out there. Do you have a fever? You've never asked to go hiking before. Only threw out some off-the-wall excuses of why you can't when I've asked. But okay. If you really want to, there's a great little trail that's pretty easy that we could . . . "

"No. I don't want to do some great little easy stupid trail. Everybody does trails. I want to make my own path. I don't want to play it safe and go where everyone else goes. I don't want to see what everyone else sees. Staying on the beaten path is boring. I want to make my own path. I want to hike up the Jesus Mountain."

What I referred to as the Jesus Mountain was pretty much right out of our front door. Our house sat at the base of it. This mountain was large. Large to me, anyway. Others might consider it a hill. But for me? It's a rather large mountain. An intimidating mountain. Now, it ain't Mount Everest, but it ain't Mount Molehill, either. This is a full-fledged mountain to me.

And let's not be all Judgey McJudgester because what you call a mountain and what I call a mountain are probably two different things.

Anyway, I call it the Jesus Mountain because it just reminds me of those rugged, sturdy mountains you see in the old Charlton Heston days of Jesus movies. You know, the movies where the men would be in their sandals, long robes, and really bad hair while holding their walking sticks in the course of making strides up a mountain? That's what it has reminded me of since we moved out here. So, ever since then, it's known as the Jesus Mountain.

And because I can see that mountaintop from most any point in the area I travel, I knew should I ever find myself lost, I can just look to the Jesus Mountain and it will lead me home.

From our house, looking from outside the hike to the mountaintop, it appeared rough and jagged and extremely rigid. Cliffs that seemed unreachable. Craggy terrain with many rough rocks, with some areas appearing difficult and unforgiving.

Between you and me, I was certain I would never make it to the top. But at least I could say I tried. No way would I allow myself to look toward the Jesus Mountain after that day and hear myself say, "I wish I would've . . . " or, "Why didn't I . . . ?"

Once I confirmed that I did indeed want to take a hike, but at my pace, Keith rolled his eyes and immediately shuffled to his closet and quickly started lacing up his worn-to-the-bone hiking boots before I could change my mind. I know he was certain at any moment I was sure to yell out, "Sucker! Just kidding . . . let's go get breakfast."

Twenty minutes and three dazzling, glossy coats of Puckering Peach later, we were headed out the door. Me, in my shiny, hardly ever worn black hiking boots and Keith with his backpack that held every imaginable first aid item created. Band-Aids. Some kind of ointment. Bug spray. Bottles of water. Toilet paper. Uh huh . . . toilet paper. He's always prepared. One of the many reasons I do love my Boy Scout.

We climbed. We trekked. We traipsed.

He encouraged. He reassured. He motivated.

I fussed. I cursed. I reapplied.

But a few hours later, we made it to the top.

I made it to the top.

And as I wiped the sweat from my neck, delicately pulled a cactus quill from gloves while asking if he packed any snacks, I stood atop of the Jesus Mountain and looked back toward our house.

I noticed how small the house and surrounding area now appeared. That old tree in the backyard was now barely visible. The broad, barren creek that for many years etched its path behind our house now seemed like a small, lonely, dry brook.

As I looked back over the side of the mountain, I saw it appeared to have a hilly flow to it. Soft curves and easy slopes. Nothing too mean and cruel. Small, colorful blooms of all shades releasing pleasant scents that somehow I had never noticed before.

And so, this is what looking from *inside* the hike to the mountaintop is like.

Once I found myself inside the hike looking out to a place I considered to be very familiar to me, it now appeared to be nothing like what I previously thought.

Even though everything was the same, everything seemed different.

Because I have been blessed with adventures I never really asked for and some I didn't even want, I'm seeing they were bestowed on me for my benefit.

They make me see who I really am and what I can really do. And they make me see me through a different pair of eyes. A pair of eyes that no longer critiques me as often as before and seems to like the girl who is learning to make this life a great adventure.

And living it.

Now, don't get me wrong. All this kayaking and hiking I do isn't every day. Or every month, for that matter. And you will certainly not find my smiling face in the dictionary under the definition of athletic.

Though I do consider myself quite a competitive one. But athletic? I think not.

Not all of life's adventures need to involve sweat. Heck, most of mine don't.

Some of my best adventures have been simply taking the doors off of my Jeep. Not worrying about what my hair looks like. Packing a bottle of water or two, a lounge chair, a good book, then finding a little hidden piece of nature to hide and read.

Or just sit and gaze at Mother Nature while watching the day pass. And hear God's whispers.

Your adventures are your own. When you find yourself smiling at you, there's an adventure you're making. When you find yourself laughing at you, high-fiving you, beaming with pride at you? More adventures are being made.

Some of your best adventures won't even appear to be adventures until you've tackled them.

They may even disguise themselves as burdens. Hardships. Or even giant misfortunes.

Like you've heard me say before, it took a little while for me to get completely on board with a move to this small border town. At that time, never would I have considered that an adventure. No way. It seemed to be more like a punishment. And for what . . . I had no idea.

The first time Keith and I visited the area to determine if I could call it home, I cried.

I cried because it was paltry. It was dirty. It was poor. It just looked pitiful. For Heaven's sake, there were chickens running loose in a few front yards. And then across the road.

This job and this move may have been his lifelong dream, but it was sure to be a nightmare for me.

There were no busy shopping centers. No noisy nail salons. No large movie theaters. Only three plain restaurants, two quiet gas stations, one meager market, and don't even think about finding any partridge or a pear tree in this place.

I didn't ask for this adventure. And I certainly didn't want this adventure.

But that was me looking from *outside* this small border town.

However, before wholly nixing the idea of ever calling this place home, I heard myself very quietly ask me, "But are you happy with the life you're living?"

And at that time, I thought I was. Heck, I knew I was! I had everything I could ever need. Traffic. Lots and lots of traffic. A miserably long work commute. A cold, lifeless cubicle I spent eight hours a day in doing a job that left me with zero satisfaction. Friends who I never seemed to have time to see. A house that always needed cleaning. Always feeling broke. Never enough time to get anything done and certainly not much time for just me. And before I knew it, another week was staring at me ready to be started. And I hadn't even finished everything I needed to do from the previous week.

Man, I was living the dream. What more could a girl ask for?

But because I have learned through the years that life ain't no dress rehearsal, and you get one shot and one shot only at it, maybe this move could be doable. If I absolutely hated it, we'd do something different. It's not like it's a forever thing anyway, right? What could it hurt? Plus, I will not finish life hearing myself say, "I wish I would've . . . " or, "Why didn't I . . . ?"

So I did.

After some time and a willing heart, convincing myself this isn't the end of the world, and with lots of praying, I discovered a few things about this small border town that I never expected to find.

Though it may not have busy shopping centers, it does have everything I need. Lots of smiles. Plenty of hugs. Many kind words. It has no strangers. Tipped hats, manners the rest of the world has forgotten, and sweet blessings are in abundance.

There may not be large movie theaters, but there are more exciting scenes than any screen could hold. The amazing sunrises. Cunning wildlife. Untouched nature presenting paths and trails some eyes have never seen. Cascading mountains that go on for what seems forever, bustling river rapids, and you can hear God whisper with each sobering breeze.

And after all of this, if you still absolutely must have a noisy nail salon, there's one about two hours down the highway. It makes for a great, occasional daytrip. And Ken does a new set of nails like nobody's business, I might add.

And so now I see this is what looking from the *inside* of this small border town is like.

I've learned that sometimes the very thing that seems as though it couldn't possibly be enough turns out to be more than enough.

Once I found myself inside this small border town, rather than just looking at it from the outside, it now appeared to be nothing like what I previously thought.

Even though everything was the same, everything seemed different.

So much of what we don't ask for but yet find ourselves saddled with turns out to be better for us than we ever thought. Don't spend your days saying, "It doesn't matter . . . whatever you want to do." It does matter. You matter. Don't allow yourself to take the backseat to anything. Don't just exist. Don't put yourself on hold, and don't watch life roll by. And for goodness sake, don't just sit on the sidelines of life for someone else's dreams. If you do, it's your own fault.

Remember, life should be a *mission* . . . not an intermission. Don't expect to find your happiness by waiting on the bench for someone else's. For one day, you're going to wake up to find all that time you just knew you had . . . is no more.

For me, and I bet you'll agree . . . life can be very much like the river. Rough and demanding and rushing.

It can also seem to be much like the Jesus Mountain. Rocky and unreachable and unforgiving.

And like the small border town? Oh, yes . . . every bit of paltry and dirty and poor.

But if we can somehow make ourselves look at life from *inside* of life rather than from the *outside* of life, we'll see that it can be beautiful and soothing and soft. It is colorful, with many kind words, and it has sweet blessings in abundance.

So be bold and make some changes if you need, regarding the negative things and unfavorable people who leave you feeling empty. Don't always play it safe. Live a little on the edge. Sometimes, just be a rebel. Do the unexpected. Try something new for the first time. Dare yourself to go big or go home.

Maybe take a few college classes. Go on that first date. Make a career change. Start planning that dream vacation. Sign up for that softball team.

Write your book.

Go deep and search for that great adventure. You may find that adventure is so heavily buried in anger and heartache and disappointment and defeat and self-destruction that it takes attempt after attempt to uncover it. But keep after it. Take baby steps. Don't throw in the towel. That adventure is so worth finding.

And when you do find it, you will see a side of your life, a life you considered to be a very familiar life to you, will now appear to be nothing like what you thought.

And even though everything will seem the same, everything will be different.

I pray you never hear yourself say, "I wish I would've . . . " or, "Why didn't I . . . ?"

For one day, you may wake up to find all that time you just knew you had . . . is no more.

Make your life a great adventure.

And go live it.

PROVERBS 16:9

The heart of man plans his way,
but the Lord establishes his steps.

CHAPTER 8

THE SIMPLEST THINGS IN LIFE ARE THE EASIEST THINGS TO UNDERSTAND, AS WELL AS THE EASIEST THINGS TO OFFER.

"**K**indness is the only language the deaf can hear and the blind can see."

I believe Mark Twain said that. Not to me personally . . . no. I never met the man. However, I am not so sure those aren't the truest words ever spoken.

Now, it's a known fact, and a fact we are at times quite proud of, but not only do we do things a tad different down here in the South, but we also say things a tad different as well.

Like, take, for instance, our words. Most of our words have a complimentary extra syllable or two added to them. Free of charge. And I say, *our words*—make sure you used two syllables each for "ow-wer" and "wer-erds"—again, I say our words because the majority of the rest of the population doesn't say things quite as we do. Some say we have a drawl. Or a twang. Or an accent. We do not. It's all of them folks who have the drawls and twangs and accents. We speak just fine, thank you very much.

And speaking of speaking . . . us southern girls speak much, much faster than the rest of the world. With Keith being from West

Texas, an area I don't hardly consider to bleed too much southern blood, and me being from southeast Texas, where our veins drip with sweet tea or homemade gravy, depending on our cholesterol levels, it's not unusual for me to do my best to finish his comments and sentences because I've got things to do. I mean, come on, sweets, I only have so much time in my day. I have heard myself say more than once, "I can say in three minutes what it takes him at least a month of Sundays to get out!"

Growing up, I think it's safe for me to say I heard it all. Between my momma and my aunts and my grandmothers, it was said. And said. And said again. I can't tell you how many times I've heard Momma say, "Do that again and I'll slap you clear into next week, little girl."

And then there's my favorite: "Would you just act like you got some sense for a change?!?"

And you just let one of us kids be suspected of doing something we had no business doing. We knew if the culprit wasn't immediately exposed, we were all going down. It was a known fact, fair or not, my grandmother was the judge and the jury. So anytime one of us kids hollered out first, "It wasn't me! I didn't do it!" you can bet the next words out of her mouth were, "The guilty dog always barks the loudest!" And sweet Jesus, she was always right.

However, there is one thing I have heard over and over for the majority of my southern aging years. And not only have I heard it, I now hear myself saying it. And that is:

"Pretty is as pretty does."

And it took me ages to ever understand just what that really means. And because my momma and my aunts and my grandmothers so often repeated those words to me as I was blossoming into a young representation of this family, I just assumed that *I* was who pretty is.

And with that, I am perfectly fine. Us girls down south find being referred to as pretty much more flattering than most anything else. I'll take *pretty* over *sweet stuff* any day. And if I'm the first to tell you, so be it. But if any boy calls you "sweet stuff" in public, you can bet his momma did not raise him right. Bless his little should know better heart. I don't care just how cute-as-a-button he is. Now, he can call you "sugar" . . . just not "sweet stuff." There is a difference. But if he does call you "sweet stuff," you can bet he was raised with the wolves. And that is not somebody you wanna hitch your wagon to.

But just what is it that *pretty* does?

Pretty puts on shiny lipstick. Because let's be honest here, we do not go to town without anything less than lipstick on our porcelain, freshly scrubbed face. If we do, that's a guarantee we will see everyone we know in the whole town, and they're all gonna be asking how your momma and 'em are doing. And do not make the mistake of the whole town seeing you with no color on those lips. Because then later, when the whole town sees your momma and 'em, they'll be asking her about your health. Because *she seemed a bit pale and faded*. And then Momma and 'em will be calling with all kinds of questions that one simple application of Blushing Begonia could have avoided.

Pretty fluffs her hair. Because, come on. We all know the higher the hair, the closer to God. Tease it to Jesus. Everybody knows everything is bigger here in the South. And if anyone ever tells you your hair is anything less than pure perfection, even if it does need a good shampooin', get rid of them. Nobody needs that kind of negativity in their life. They should lie to you if they have to. Why, one of the best compliments you can give a southern woman is, "Honey, that is some southern hair if I've ever seen it!" Even if it is frizzy from this atrocious humidity we fight daily. There is not one of us that wouldn't simply beam hearing those words. If you don't own a teasing comb with the spikes that could maim an intruder and a can of hair spray strong enough to fill a pothole in the road, try as you might, you are not really from these parts.

Pretty polishes her nails. Just because. That's why. No real reason needed. You just cannot be out and about with chipped-up nails. On either end. Toes are included here. It can be found in the book of Carrie 3:14, "Thou must always be pristinely polished from tips to toenails because your radiant personality isn't always the first thing noticed." Period. And it does say it. Look it up if you must.

But after so many years of hearing, "Pretty is as pretty does," I started to learn that *pretty* is not really me.

No. It's not me at all.

Oh, there might be days I feel pretty. Or even think I look pretty. But pretty isn't a thing. It isn't an unveiling or a debut or a display.

Being pretty or not has nothing to do with appearance, but it has everything to do with how you make others feel.

Oh, wait. Before I forget, let me tell you a story I heard from a preacher man years ago that has stuck with me. Then we'll get back to gabbing about what pretty is.

This story? It hit me right in that hollow spot, and it has lived there ever since.

It was about an old Indian chief.

When the lands were barren and the rains were desperately needed by the townspeople, they would always reach out to this old Indian chief. For it was known, every time he did his rain dance, the rains would come.

Without fail . . . when he danced, it rained.

One of the townspeople decided to visit with him one day to seek out his secret. It had been happening for years, and he wanted to know why. What was this old Indian chief's secret to consistently bringing the rains?

"Every time you do a rain dance, it rains. How is that? What is your secret? Why do the rains always respond to your dance?"

"That's easy," the old chief replied. "It rains every time I dance because I dance until it rains."

Well, now that puts a whole new spin on it, don't you think?

I've always just loved that story and wanted to tell it to you. It'll make more sense why I just had to throw that out to you in a bit.

So, moving right along . . . where were we? Oh, yes . . . we were talking about what pretty does.

Pretty might do a lot of things. And most of those things don't really mean a hill of beans to anyone.

Pretty may put on shiny lipstick.

And pretty may fluff her hair to the high heavens and polish her nails.

But the one most important thing pretty does?

Pretty rains.

Pretty isn't what you are.

Pretty isn't who you are.

Pretty isn't just a feeling you have.

Pretty isn't the best French manicure this side of the Mississippi.

Pretty is an affection.

Pretty is an affection *you rain upon others.*

We all know that someone who is simply stunning to look at. Perfectly coiffed hair. The most magnificent eyelashes you've ever seen. She has mastered the art of liquid eyeliner like nobody's business.

Then Miss Priss opens her mouth. And she speaks through her exquisitely lined, pouty lips.

Gasp. Ugh. Oooohh. No, thank you.

Her arrogance fills the room. Her audacity simply bewilders. Her confidence stems from her conceitedness that leaves you certain of one thing: beauty *is* truly found only in the eye of the beholder.

She's rude. She's belittling. She's pompous. She is just not your kind of sweet tea.

But that eyeshadow? Oh, heavens how does she ever perfect such a smoky and sultry look?

Her mannerisms, her actions toward others, and her demeaning attitude immediately diminish her beauty. She's not so pretty anymore. Those pristinely polished nails aren't even noticed. And those eyebrows don't seem so superbly arched anymore. She's, well

. . . she's just plain ol' ugly.

Just as ugly as homemade sin.

Poor thing. She couldn't find her rain if it bit her in the . . . never mind. Don't get me cursing.

And there are always those few who think being allowed in the holy circle of losers of Miss Priss actually makes them worthy. And they'll always defend her hideous ways with, "Well, once you get to know her, she's really sweet."

Really?

So, in other words, until *you* make the effort to get to know *her*, she's just gonna be a big ol' . . . well, not so sweet girl?

I never realized being kind was something you had to forage for in others. Something hidden and deeply buried for you to find.

And let me confess right now. Hear me and hear me good: I ain't doing it. Oh, don't get wrong, if I just look up and there she is and I don't have time to turn and run into the ladies' room or hide in a closet, I'll smile and say hello. If for no other reason than because my momma raised me better. And it has been said the best test for good manners is the ability to be patient with bad ones. In other words, kill 'em with kindness then bury 'em with a smile. But there's not enough time in my life to devote to trying to befriend the ill-mannered like that. No way, no how. And you're not gonna make me.

No. Instead, I'd rather just pray for her.

Over the years, no matter how hard I've tried to find some pretty in everyone, I've come to realize not everyone has some pretty to be found. Maybe it can be found by others, just not by me. And I'll make tons of excuses for them such as, *"Oh, maybe he's just having a tough time on the job."* That's when the rather unfantastic side of me responds with, *"Well, if that's the case, he's been having a tough time for months now. By the way, is he still rolling his eyes and heavily sighing during those staff meetings?"*

Or I'll try to convince myself, *"Maybe she's having health problems I don't know anything about."* And then I hear myself reply to me with,

"Seems like any health problems she's having she's been having since grade school. Remember that dodgeball game where you were her only target?"

But have you ever noticed how some people, no matter how pretty or not they may already be, just seem to get prettier by their actions and the words they simply rain upon you and others?

I was circling the parking lot of the little shopping area in my small border town last Christmas. It was packed. Tourists, visitors, family from out of town spending time with family in town. Folks from the other side of nowhere vacationing on this side of nowhere. People were just everywhere. Cars were flowing from end to end waiting for other shoppers to vacate a parking spot. I was on the verge of just throwing my hands up and returning later. However, I was not going to let all this mess ruin my festive mood! I would just leave and knock out a few other errands I had on my list.

Then, lo and behold, there it was. I swore I heard the angels humming. And humming loud. I saw an empty parking spot! I finally must have been living right! Thank you, Jesus! For there it was in all of its empty paint-chipped, curb-stop, oil-stained, and asphalt glory. And right by the front doors at that. It was perfect.

Well, perfect except for the fact there was a man standing in the middle of it. Apparently saving it. No doubt he was saving it for some poor fool who had been circling already way too long and was slowly, but surely, losing that holiday festive spirit.

Still, though. I couldn't believe it. Saving an empty parking spot down here in the South is right up there with saving a seat in church.

You just don't do it.

Now, as you can imagine, there are plenty of things in this world that ruffle my feathers. Not saying thank you and just walking on by when I hold the door for you. Or giving me directions using east or west. No, don't embarrass yourself with that silly talk. It's "take a left at the Walmart," not "turn east on Main Street."

But to save a seat in church? Are you kidding me? Nowhere in my

Bible have I read when Jesus was speaking to the masses and some poor soul wanted to join the crowds and hear what He had to say did anyone lean over to the newcomer and in a little too loud whisper speak the words, "I'm sorry, this seat is saved."

Hearing those very words have made me say things to myself that no church-going southern woman should ever have to utter to herself. Especially right there in the center aisle of the church when she was denied seating by some ill-mannered grandma thinking the grandkids and cousins were actually gonna do their once-a-year show up for Christmas services.

Anyway, back to that miraculously empty parking spot.

Now, when I saw that man standing there, saving that spot like he didn't have the sense God gave a goose, don't think I didn't grumble a bit to myself. Of course I did. I was a woman on a mission in a shopping center at Christmas time, for festive sake. But I'd just keep circling and find another spot. One saved parking spot was not going to ruin my day.

Now, I will admit, when it comes to getting a parking spot, we women pull out all the stops. If Keith was with me, I would've probably made him get out and walk the lot scoping out exiting shoppers. You know, so I could sit in my car in the lane just behind them as they were loading bags into their backseat, blocking any traffic behind me from going around, with my blinker on showing any and every one I was planning to turn into this exact spot the second they moved. All the while, my hand placed firmly on the horn. Why? Because I'd be daring other circling drivers that might be coming toward me with my glaring smile to not even think about pulling in that spot ahead of me. That would get them a quick ticket to see Jesus. But never would I act like I knew him if he actually stepped foot in that empty spot and stood there. I'd just glare at him through my window as I drove on by. How utterly embarrassing.

Next thing I knew, this man started waving at me. At least I thought it was me. I turned and looked around and, well, I was the only vehicle *right there* in his line of sight. Actually, he wasn't waving

. . . it was more like he was motioning at me. Motioning for me to turn into that gloriously empty parking spot right by the front doors.

So, with a big smile, and forgetting how I'd rightfully so write Keith out of my will should he ever do this, I gladly made that left turn.

As I put it in park and turned off the ignition, in no time, he was at my door opening it. And it was then I recognized him. This was the brother of Keith's coworker who I had met several weeks before. I guess with all the congestion in the parking lot, me busy using a few un-festive words to myself about the festive holiday shoppers not watching where they were festively walking, I just didn't recognize him!

As I climbed out of my car, in his very broken English, he says, "*Hola*, Ms. Carrie! I see you driving and looking for a place to park. So busy and so many people. I park over there and come save this for you!"

"Well, aren't you just the nicest thing? You just made my day . . . I owe you a Coke for this!"

We laughed, and I gave him a hug. I then asked how his momma and 'em were doing, inquired about any holiday travels he may have planned, wished him a *Feliz Navidad*, then thanked him profusely as he held open the entrance door to the holiday shoppers' haven for me.

I couldn't thank him enough for his undue kindness.

But what did I really want to do?

Cry a little.

Why?

Because he could have simply parked his own car, locked the doors, and strolled on inside to get his shopping started. Plus, it was rather chilly out, and he wasn't wearing much more than a light jacket. He could have just thought nothing of seeing me circling, because no doubt, he himself did his fair share of circling. He could have never given me a second thought. We could have visited inside and exchanged our greetings there.

However, he chose, without expecting anything in return, to make my day a little brighter. With a little rain. I didn't ask for it. I didn't anticipate it. And at the time, I didn't even realize it or want it, for that matter. But he offered it. He found me worthy of a little of his kindness. A scant raining of his "pretty," if you will.

And just what did that do? It put me smack dab in the middle of being festive and kind to others.

Because I danced until it rained.

I do believe I wished more people a Merry Christmas or a *Feliz Navidad* on that one day than I did all season!

But I'm seeing just like it's so easy to drench some ugly on others when you've had some ugly drenched on you, it's just as easy to rain a storm of pretty. Plus, it makes you feel better. About you and about life, in general.

I don't know about you, but when hard days wake me up, pull me out of bed, and glare at me? And when absolutely nothing goes right? And when I'm certain I have been declared society's local whipping post? The last thing I'm in the mood to do is dance. And if I do dance, I ain't dancing for long. During those down days and low spots in life, the most difficult thing for me to do is keep a smile on my face. I don't want to talk. I don't want to laugh. I don't want to breathe. I don't want to visit. I don't want to like people. And I certainly don't want to smile.

But you know what? If I fake the smile and make myself smile on purpose, when that's really the last thing I want to do, the majority of the time, I'll get that smile rained right back on me. And it's not unusual for the incoming smile to splash me with a little kindness that's attached to it, as well. And no matter how small that splash of kindness is, it's sometimes still too much for me to keep a hold of. And before I know it, I find myself splashing it on someone else.

Because I danced until it rained.

Like that time I was cruising the card aisles at the dollar store. Minding my own, mad at the world, business. And who knows why I was mad? And more importantly, just why was I looking at cards? Heck, I don't know. I don't know why I do a lot of things I do. But I can tell you one thing: I did not want to speak to anyone. But I was at least putting forth an effort and making myself smile. I was not in the mood to even fake that smile I was smiling, but I was smiling. And I especially was not in the mood to smile at or deal with that little old man shuffling behind his buggy headed straight toward me. And let me tell you, it was clear the only thing keeping him upright was that buggy.

I quickly told myself, *Just lay low and don't make eye contact. He'll mind his own business and go on by.* Plus, he was moving slower than molasses traveling uphill. I'd have every card read and reread by the time he shuffled himself all the way down this aisle.

"Excuse me, little lady?"

In my head to me, and thank goodness only to me, I barked out the words, *Well, son of a gun. I guess I'm going to hell in a handbasket. So much for my stupid plan of laying low. Apparently, Jesus is punishing me now, and I reckon I'm gonna have to not only smile but speak as well.*

I looked up at him with my fake smile. It was a very forced smile and not very pretty, of that I am sure.

His face was weathered. His hand shook as he reached out to me. Though his English was considerably clear, make no bones about it, Spanish was his first language.

Though he had to be no less than a million years old, his eyes were sincere, and his smile was genuine. He was every bit of a towering five feet tall. And I know that because we were eye to eye with each other. Though I stood up straight, he had a slight tilt forward.

As my hand reached his enticing grip, he let go of his trusty buggy and laid his free hand on top of mine. What an immense sign of trust he was awarding me. But this seemed more than just a simple handshake to this old man. No, this was a heartfelt embrace.

"My name is Alfredo. You can remember my name because everyone likes Alfredo noodles. Everyone! But noodles is not my last name. Call me Alfredo, little lady. I am an old man who must send a card to his sister. Please choose one for me. Any card you like will be just fine, and it will be the one I shall send to her."

And sweet heavens above, how could I not agree to read a card or two to an old man? I mean, I might not have been having the best day, but I'm not evil, for Heaven's sake.

I read him a few cards. We took our own sweet time and decided on one together. I didn't realize it at the time, but I wasn't putting the rush on, and I found myself actually enjoying our conversation. And I was smiling. And what's even better? It wasn't fake, and it wasn't forced. It was all coming natural. Alfredo and his rains of kindness, or pretty if you will, was slowly changing my mad at the world mood.

During our small talk, I learned it was his younger sister's birthday, but any nice card would do. We decided on one that expressed she was very special and thought of often.

He thanked me for helping him choose, and he tossed the card in his buggy.

Before he shuffled off back down the aisle, I then leaned toward him, smiled, and hugged his neck. My goodwill was returned with a kiss on the cheek. I've come to learn this is a gentlemanly trait many elderly Hispanic men still offer. Then he kindly thanked me for my time.

It was then he pointed a frail, crooked, wrinkled finger at me and said with a sincere air, "I am an old man who has seen a lot in his lifetime. Your time is important to you, and you just gave some of your time to this old man. I thank you for that, little lady."

I couldn't help but notice his World War II veteran cap he so proudly wore atop of his now small, fragile frame. A frame, I'm sure, that was once solid and strong. Brimming with a soldier's endurance and stamina not too many today could comprehend. Capable of hauling weapons, clothes, food, and whatever else was needed to win the war. Never mind the ability to carry a wounded, or let alone much worse, fellow fighter.

I heard myself chuckle with a slight blush. I then said to him, "It has been my pleasure. Visiting with you has made my day much brighter than it started out being. I hope your sister likes her card. She is very lucky to have a big brother like you. So, I see your cap.

Thank you for your service, Alfredo."

"Thanks is not needed. I love my country. I leave my mother and family right here in this town when I was just a boy to serve my country. Me, along with my six brothers, were in World War II. I fight, I serve, and then I come home. As did all of my brothers. After World War II, we all go to Korea. My mother was so very sad to see us all once again leave to fight in a war. But it's what we all wanted to do. We love our country. But it was Korea not all of my brothers returned home. But, little lady, I am a blessed man in many ways. Not many have been given ninety-two years on this earth as I have been. Now, you do this old man a favor. Go home and have yourself a shot of whiskey for this old veteran. Have two if you'd like!"

At that time, it was pouring. The rains had come. A gully washer was more like it. Alfredo had rained so much of his pretty on me I was now overflowing with an abundance of kindness. As well as a few tears. It was too much for me to handle all on my own; I had to give some away. So, as I checked my items and paid the cashier, I bought her a Coke and some M&Ms, and I freely gave her an unforced smile.

Because I danced until it rained.

The smile she returned came with an expression of surprise and a kind word of thanks. She then greeted her next customer in line with a rather enthusiastic grin. Not the weary and worn one she welcomed me with.

Each Sunday morning at church, Alfredo is seated in the last row. And each Sunday morning at church, I lean down to hug his neck, ask him to please stay seated, and he kisses my cheek. And I then share his rain of pretty with others.

So, back to that question of just what does "pretty" do.

Yes, pretty may put on shiny lipstick.

And pretty may fluff her hair to the high heavens and polish her nails.

But remember, pretty isn't who you are. Or what you are.

Pretty isn't a feeling you have.

Pretty is much, much more than that.

Pretty is an affection.

Pretty is an affection *you rain upon others.*

And sometimes, the rains aren't there. You don't feel the rain, and you don't see the rain.

But just like the old Indian chief, you dance. And you dance. And you dance some more.

You dance until it rains.

You see, the simplest things in life are the easiest things to understand, as well as the easiest things to offer.

A smile. A hug. A handshake. A saved parking spot.

A simple kiss on the cheek.

Things like these are a language we all understand regardless of the language we speak.

From back when I was knee-high to a grasshopper, I've always reminded myself that whenever I must choose between doing what is right or doing what is kind. Always choose kindness. The world has plenty of right, but never can it have enough kindness.

For never have I thought to myself, *Sweet heavens, that lady sure is right!*

But I have thought, *My goodness, what a kind heart that is.*

Because kindness is the only language the deaf can hear and the blind can see. And we all can understand.

And though we may forever have our shiny lipstick and our perfectly coiffed hair fluffed to the high heavens and our pristinely polished nails . . . kindness is the only thing that really makes us pretty.

Because pretty really is as pretty really does.

HEBREWS 13:2

Do not neglect to show hospitality to strangers,
for by this some have entertained angels
without knowing it.

• CHAPTER 9 •

A GOOD FRIEND? THEY KNOW YOUR STORY. BUT A BEST FRIEND? THEY HELP YOU WRITE YOUR STORY.

O
h, she was nice and all.

For the most part, anyway.

I mean, people seemed to like her. I don't know many who didn't, actually. She was always smiling and had a cheerful attitude. She somehow had a way of very easily meeting people. Her laugh could be contagious. And her sense of humor? Extraordinary, to say the least. With no effort at all, she could light up a room.

Just for some reason, I found myself simply tolerating her most of the time. I could never determine exactly what it was others saw in her. Because I certainly didn't see it.

I'm pretty sure we all have an acquaintance or four we seem to tolerate more than we actually like. I mean, it's not that there's anything you *don't* like about them. You just can't pinpoint what it is that you *do* like about them.

I've always felt I have tons of acquaintances but very few friends. And I'm not so certain I'd go as far as to say any *best* friends. Oh, now I do have a few good friends . . . but best friends? I'm not sure I can honestly crown anyone with that title.

And speaking of friends, there's a big difference between a good friend and a best friend, you know?

A good friend? They know your story.

But a best friend? They help you write your story.

Anyway, I've known her for what seems like forever. And most of the time, we mixed like oil and water. We just never saw eye to eye with each other. Well, we seemed to do better when we were younger. But as we got a little older . . . she kept me in a constant state of eye rolling. And sighing. And mumbling words no church-going girl should mumble. It always seemed like she was on a constant crash course of finding perfection. More in herself than with others.

And that perfection she was searching for? I told her time and time again she'd never find it. Perfection is not out there. And you'd think by the time she was in her twenties, she'd understand no one is perfect. For Heaven's sake, every dog has a few fleas. But this girl? Hardheaded. She never listened. She always thought she knew what was best for her and Heaven forbid she listen to anyone else.

She is the very reason I came to understand what my daddy meant when, growing up, he called me "stubborn as an old mean mule."

And Lord have mercy, I'll never understand why I tried so hard with her. You know, sometimes you really can't explain just what it is you see in a person. I think it's the way they take you to a place no one else can. She did that for me. It's like I was afraid for her to be alone. Maybe I was just dimwitted enough to think I could save her from herself. Who knows?

More than once, I wanted to tell her to take a long walk off a short pier. She was ornery. She was relentless. She was, at most times, selfish. However, she could also be quite subtle. As a roaring freight train! And my goodness, could she pitch one fine hissy fit when the mood hit her. But for some reason, when she'd want to talk, I'd always listen to her and then offer my advice. Advice she asked for but never appreciated, much less took. I should have hit the floor running like a scalded dog when I had the chance.

Like the time I told her this guy was not the guy for her and she should really do some soul searching and praying. Something deep down inside told me he was just not her Mr. Right she so strongly thought he was.

So what did she go and do?

She up and married him.

Oh, yes, she did.

Why did I think he wasn't the one for her? I don't rightly know. It was more of a gut feeling, I guess. Maybe God was whispering to me? Women's intuition, maybe? I couldn't put my finger on it, but I just knew he wasn't her Mr. Right. Or even her Mr. Kinda Maybe Right.

Now, I'm no handsomely bald Kojak who can solve cases from sea to shining sea in one sultry, adventurous one-hour Saturday night episode. But it might've had something to do with the fact he had been unfaithful to his first wife. More than once. His wife. The mother of his two children. That alone should have been a big fat red flag. I mean, my goodness! Did she think she wasn't worthy of something better than that? Did she not feel she deserved an honest man who could at least be faithful? But even after I threw those questions at her, all I got back was, "He'll be different with me . . . I'm not like her, anyway. Plus, all my friends are getting married and having babies. It's my turn!"

Once she made her decision that she was indeed going to walk down that aisle, I didn't hear much from her. She was busy wedding planning and didn't seem to need time with me anymore. And between you and me, I know she had to know better. She was raised to make better decisions than this.

Plus, there was nothing I could say or do to convince her otherwise. Deep in my heart, I knew she had to recognize she was heading in the wrong direction. But would she admit it? No way, no how. She insisted she knew what was best for her, and that's that. Discussions closed. However, I may or may not have reminded her numerous times, "The sun don't shine on the same dog's tail all the time." Meaning, we all get what we deserve sooner or later in life. And she needed to remember that. And you know I'm right. It happens to the best of us whether we like it or not. Some call it Karma.

I should've ditched her right then and there.

It wasn't too terribly long before she remembered where to find me. And before I realized it, I was still around and listening to all her babbling when she was quite upset, to say the least. Why? Well, her so-called Mr. Right, who she just had to run down the aisle with, had decided to accept a new job offer.

That probably sounds like no big deal. But it was. It was hours away. Like a full day's drive number of hours away. You heard me. Hours away from where they had just built a perfect little house. Started a new little life. And here's the best part: she could certainly go with him if she wanted or she could just come to visit him on weekends.

Excuse me, but what the what? Visit on the weekends? Well, doesn't that just take the cake? Bless his sweet little heart! He was considerate enough to understand she may not want to leave her career she had been building and start over in a new city. Even though he already decided to take a job a day's drive away from where he already had a perfectly fine job. You know, hours away from where they were starting this new life together? God love him. What a gem, he was! Every girl should be so lucky!

Ehem. Where's my wine?

I tried to explain to her she was getting the short end of the stick in this deal. Didn't she think she deserved a little more respect than this? Why should she have to leave what she's been building just to better his career? This was not part of the deal when they married. Was there no happy medium to be found? I mean, I went so far as to remind her of those silly vows apparently only she took in that marriage. You know the ones. For richer or for poorer? Doesn't that basically mean you stick together and at least discuss what might be best for both and not what might be best for one? And you surely don't go making decisions and taking job offers without arguing about it first! And I mean big decisions. Not little stuff like whether you want two or three lumps of sugar in your coffee.

And what about that scripture that says something about how a man is united to his wife and they become one flesh? I know it's in the first book of the Bible, the one about Adam and Eve, but I was so mad all I could remember was the one in Carrie 3:28 that says, "Lord, please give me patience, because if you give me strength, I'm gonna need bail money to go with it!"

Thank heavens, for what I do believe was the first time ever, she actually listened to what I was saying. My words finally penetrated her thick head. Hallelujah, she heard me. She let my words soak in. She thought about it, and she prayed about it. And she came to her decision about it.

She promptly left her career and moved with him so he could better his.

Well, son of a gun.

I made myself live with her ridiculous decision no matter how stupid I thought it was. And I simply thought it was stupid because there was no discussion or negotiations or anything about it. Not even a good old fashioned, door-slamming, shoe-throwing brawl. It was his way or the highway.

If I didn't know better, I'd think she was on her very own personal highway to Hell just to simply punish herself. After a bit, this seemed so self-inflicted. Like she thought she deserved such heartache. And for what? I don't even think she knew.

I was so angry with her I wanted to spit.

And come to think about it, I'm pretty sure I did. Several times.

We didn't talk too terribly much once she moved. And that was just fine by me. Oh, I'd hear from her every now and then, but it was mostly to prove to me how wrong I was about her decision and how I should really be more open-minded. She did her best to show me just how ecstatically happy she was. Life was just so grand! I mean, the sun comes up just to hear her crow!

Liar.

She was good at most everything she did. Except lying, mind you.

I could see right through her false words and fake smiles. They say you should always keep your friends close and your enemies closer. And I simply kept her close because I just never knew which part she was playing. My friend? Or my enemy? I suppose it depended on her mood that day.

I would always tell myself to *be the old lady who fell out of the wagon* when she'd come back around and start bending my ear again. In other words, "If you aren't involved and it doesn't concern you, keep your nose out of it because it's none of your business." This was her mess she was constantly making, and she could waller around in it if she wanted, but keep me far away.

I should have seen this coming, but before I knew it, she was talking babies.

Never mind she married a man who was unfaithful and self-serving. Never mind she married a man who she was starting to see as inconsiderate and deceptive. She admitted she couldn't trust him as far as she could throw him. Their marriage was spent more time apart than together. His job consisted of weeks of travel. Her job didn't allow her the time to go with him. Many days and nights were spent alone. However, it seemed in her mind he was an ideal candidate to father her children. A baby would make it better.

What. A. Fool.

Again, I tried, and I tried to make her see the light. It's like I kept thinking she'd be different this time and she'd genuinely hear me and sincerely consider where her actions were taking her. I begged her to give this some time and to really think hard about bringing a baby into this marriage with this man.

Was the love there? Was the stability there? Was the commitment there?

I convinced her to talk to God. A lot. About her marriage and especially about this baby stuff. Heck, maybe He could talk some sense into her because I certainly couldn't. Maybe He could open her eyes to see the consequences of her actions. Maybe He would even consider putting this marriage on the right path and mend so much heartache. And maybe He could find some room in that marriage and be at the core of it.

Because really, I knew He was the only one that could rebuild all that was broken here.

But something had to be done.

She was becoming more than I could handle.

Or, actually, it was more like she was becoming more than I wanted to handle.

What I really wanted was to tell her to buzz off. Just leave me alone and to take her complicated life issues with her. Hit the road, Jack. I didn't have the time nor did I want to make the time to deal with her. Especially since she didn't listen to a thing I said. Messing with her was just a big waste of my sanity. My mind was made up. I was going to be as self-centered as her and tell her to just buzz off and go away.

But, well, that would be just downright ugly, now wouldn't it?

And God doesn't like ugly.

So I figured I'd just slowly distance myself from her. Be a little more difficult to find. Too busy, if you will. Playing with my own deck of cards. Not always be the old faithful and reliable moral compass she had come to rely on always being there. But the more I tried to distance myself from her and all of her issues, the more I found myself drawn to her.

It's like she was a part of me.

After many visits with her doctor, who eventually sent her to a specialist, who eventually sent her into exploratory surgery, it was confirmed there would be no babies.

She took this news hard. We pretty much ceased all talking at that point. She wanted nothing to do with anyone. Not me, not her family, and especially not God.

I had no advice. I had no suggestions. I had nothing for her.

It was her greatest heartbreak.

She did her best to trudge through life and not cry at every baby shower invitation that came through the mail. Not cry every time she saw a baby seat in a car. Not cry simply because she could.

She wasn't in control anymore. It was out of her hands. There was nothing she could do from this point on.

The plans she had made were no longer hers to make.

You know what she did? She counted her chickens before they hatched, that's what she did. And that is one thing down here in the South we are warned to never do from day one! Nothing good ever comes of it.

And if I was a betting woman, I'd say she knew this all along. It seems someone greater than her who could see down her road and knew the path He designed for her had finally taken over. Which I wish would have happened years ago.

Somehow, she was going to have to go through life with no skinned knees to kiss. There wouldn't be little toenails to polish pink. No training wheels, no bedtime stories, no class parties. Ballet lessons were out of the picture now. Forget cheering from the stands as he slid into second base.

No prom dresses. No fresh haircuts. No first dates.

No wedding gowns. No tuxedos with cummerbunds. No grandbabies.

And just when she thought life couldn't get any worse, it most certainly did.

After ten years of this so-called marriage, following his career, and praying for babies, she discovered he was having affairs.

Affairs. Plural. With an "s."

I know. I almost died for her.

Oh, he gave her every excuse in the world. Of course he did. But you know what? You can't polish a turd. And excuses? They're like backsides. Everybody's got one, and they all stink.

I say she *discovered* this, but she always had that feeling. Deep down inside, she knew. Maybe there's something to be said for that woman's intuition stuff? It was just something she kept thinking would go away if she ignored it.

But it never does, now does it?

For a while, she did her best to continue life as normal. Things would work themselves out. Things would start looking up.

Once she found herself inside looking out to a place she considered to be very familiar, it now appeared to be nothing like what she previously thought.

Even though everything was the same, everything seemed different.

This was her lowest point.

She now had even more to cry about. It seemed all she did was cry. As a matter of fact, she cried so much she couldn't find the spirit to be angry. Sweet heavens, she was so unsettled she was eating sorrow by the spoonful.

She secretly wondered if, way back when she knew he wasn't the one but yet married him anyway, if she would have listened to me, would things have turned out differently?

If she would have heeded God's whispers and warnings during all these years, would her life be on a stronger path? A more joyous and fulfilling path?

Knowing her, she'll wonder these thoughts throughout her lifetime. This will forever be her heaviest cross to bear.

I can't say we chatted much during this time. There wasn't much *we* to our *us* anymore. This time, it was more me talking to her than vice versa. She didn't say much back to me at all, and, well, she didn't even act like she heard me.

But I kept by her. I stayed with her. I couldn't leave her.

I can honestly say she didn't really like herself. She felt as if she had failed at everything she attempted. She gave her best for a faithful marriage, a blossoming career, as well as much-desired motherhood. But no. They weren't going to happen.

She knew she was a broken woman.

And I guess, in a sense, I could understand where she was coming from. But, you know, I don't think she ever stopped to think maybe it wasn't a broken future but instead a broken dream. And maybe it wasn't a broken life after all, but instead simply a broken heart.

I was going to dig her out of this hole she had gotten herself into if it was the last thing I ever did for her.

You know when you know that you just know?

I knew it was time for her to make a decision, even if it was a wrong decision. It was time. I knew it, and she knew it.

She finally concluded divorce was most likely her only option at this point. She prayed more than ever. Not for situations to work in her favor, but for her life to follow His will.

She prayed for wisdom. For the wisdom to know right from weak. She wanted to do the right thing for her life and for her future . . . not the weak, easy way out.

For strength. For the strength to hold it together when the more logical thing seemed to be to fall apart. Strength grows during the times you are certain you can't go on. But you do, anyway.

For perseverance. For the perseverance to never give up. And to remember life may get harder before it gets easier. And to keep trying. Try and try. Then try again.

But mostly, she prayed for peace.

For peace while making her decisions. For she knew if she didn't have peace when making her decisions, she'd never have peace once those decisions were made.

She discovered she will never speak to anyone more than she speaks to her soul. She learned she must speak kindness not only to others, but more so to herself. Even if it's just a whisper.

Because words that soak into your soul are whispered . . . not yelled.

Once the inevitable was placed before her, she remained civil, she remained calm, and she somehow found the courage to forge ahead.

As a divorced woman. A crown she never dreamed she'd don.

I tried to convince her this was a new beginning. A do-over. Her second chance. She could be who she wanted and do what she wanted and when she wanted. This was her life to live, and it could be as exciting as she wanted to make it. If you give life a chance, it can make greatness out of a great mess.

And really? For all she knew, she may have just been handed, quite possibly, one of the best blessings life has ever offered her.

She proceeded to build a new life in a new city. It was a slow process. It took more wisdom than she knew she had. It took a strength she never saw in herself before. It took perseverance that brought on tears, restless nights, and more ranting and raving than she'd ever done. Which let's be honest . . . ranting and raving is just a churched-up way of saying she used her limit of unladylike words. And let me tell you, some of those words she threw out there were made up as they spewed out of her shiny lips! Heck, some she didn't even know what they meant.

However, it took peace. Loads of peace. A peace she found within herself. A peace no one else could provide. A peace that had to be nurtured.

All of this was found hours away from where her previous life had started. And ended. We felt a clean slate and some time alone would be the best prescription for her.

For life to take on a new meaning and for life to be all hers, nothing but hers, she knew she had to do something that was totally out of her comfort zone.

She did what she had to do: go where the fear is.

New city. New job. New friends. New life.

After a while, I noticed she had stopped pursuing perfection. She started accepting her flaws. It was as if she was understanding her flaws weren't so much imperfections, but a makeup of who she was and who she was becoming. They were what set her apart from the rest. What made her stand out from the crowds. And, thank goodness for me, she was becoming so much easier to live with. She was happy again. Cheerful. Resilient. She was starting to understand no other person or circumstance could define her or determine her worth. Only she could do that.

She was seeing life as good again. Exciting, fun, full of energy.

It was a hard lesson for her to learn, and it most certainly dumped its fair share of heartache right in her lap, but she was finally understanding she had to learn to love herself. If she didn't love herself, she would spend her life chasing after others who didn't love her either.

Learning to love herself was her rain dance. It wasn't always an easy dance. The rain didn't always come.

But she kept at it.

She danced until it rained.

It was also becoming quite clear to her that life would never be perfect. As it shouldn't be. Where is the fun and excitement in perfection? Perfection is boring, don't you think? But however imperfect her life may be, she can still make it work.

She felt the world was watching and waiting for her to fail. Fumble the ball. Lose the game.

But she knew she couldn't tell the world her plans. If she did, it would only point and laugh. And encourage her to give up. Instead, she had to show the world her ending results.

You're probably rolling your eyes a bit and asking, "So why she didn't call her momma during these tough times? Or maybe her sister? Why did she call you? You didn't really even like each other. Why didn't she just call her best girlfriend?"

She did call her best girlfriend.

Just at the time, neither one of us realized it.

She called me because I was the only one who knew her. I knew her thoughts, her heart, her soul. I knew what upset her, and I knew what sent her spirit soaring. I knew everything about her . . . her good, her bad, and unfortunately . . . all of her ugly.

For I was her.

The very girl I never liked much or could see eye to eye with, later down the line in life, turned out to be my very best friend. She kept my deepest secrets, and she always pushed me beyond my limits.

Remember?

A good friend? They know your story.

But a best friend? They help you write your story.

You are, and will always be, your best friend. The only person you can be certain of spending the rest of your life with is you. So you better love who you are and enjoy your own company.

If you don't, no one else will, either.

So spend time with you. You're worth it and you deserve it. You give everybody else so much of your energy and time and devotion, I'm sure it may seem like there's nothing left. That's not only a disservice to them, but an even bigger disservice to you. You have to take care of yourself before you can take care of anyone else.

Learn to enjoy some time alone with yourself. Learn to understand yourself. Learn to tolerate yourself.

Go to a movie. Or supper. Or both.

Do a weekend getaway. Attend a cooking class. Or maybe a shopping spree.

Just do something for you. For only you and with only you.

Even if you just go sit quietly in the park and watch the world from a bench.

Keep searching until you discover something that brings out a spark in you. A fire deep down. Maybe even something a little crazy. Life is short. Those three little words might be the most repeated words in history, and the older you get, the truer they become. If there's ever a time to unearth and pinpoint what can be a true passion and do something you love . . . something you really, really love . . . that time is right now.

Today.

Why are we here anyway, if not to live with an exciting, soul-searing passion?

And washing clothes, doing the yard work, and pushing a buggy down the wine aisle at the grocery store will never be an exciting passion. I'm not falling for that, so find something else to argue with me about.

Don't find yourself more bitter than a lemon peel like so many and one day hear yourself whispering, "I wish I would have . . . " or, "Why didn't I . . . " It's too late, then. And if I promise you nothing else, I promise you this: that is when you'll truly know the bitter taste of regret.

Once you like you and begin to appreciate the good soul you are, you'll find yourself happier. And full of spirit. And looking for the best in others. Then finding it.

And another thing. Once you like you? You'll see there's this one thing you'll find yourself doing more than ever before. And it will be something that just comes as natural to you like pearls and peach cobbler, *yes, ma'am* and *no, sir*, and an extra layer of lip gloss comes to us girls down here in the South:

You will smile.

Because that's what we do down here in the South. We smile. A lot.

I will certainly admit, heartbreak and starting over at the same time might possibly be one of the toughest things to push through. Especially when you feel alone. And lost. And abandoned.

But you know, one day when you look back on those tough times? You're going to realize those tough times can be some of your best times.

Hang on, stay with me here. Get another glass of wine if you need to. I'll wait. And bring me one, too.

Those tough times can be some of your best times to develop your character. To strengthen your courage. To show you and everybody else just what you're made of. Don't let those hard moments go to waste just like you shouldn't let those good times go to waste. Don't let the things and happenings going on around you get inside of you. Don't let them tell the world who you are. You tell the world who you are.

For the most part, I believe my life is as good as my mindset.

There's not a day that goes by you won't be able to find some ugly in it. Trust me, we both know there are lots of ugly to be found out there these days. And yes, there are days I do find my share of it. I let something someone said, did, or didn't do get inside of me and, well, just fester. And I'd be lying if I told you there are times when I find that ugly . . . I hang on to it for hours. Sometimes for days. Why? I just want to be mad and pout. Why? I just do. I'm a redhead. I don't necessarily need a reason for much I do in life.

Go ahead. Be mad and pout. Throw a shoe or two. Not the good heels, though. Pout up a storm. Get it out. Waller in it if you want.

When I was younger and would pitch a hissy fit, first thing my momma would say, "Go ahead, little girl . . . get mad. But you just better remember you gotta get glad in those same britches you just got mad in."

Not every day is going to be working in our favor. Not everything will be coming our way. That's not really best for us, anyway . . . always getting our way. That makes us spoiled. And spoiled things don't smell too good.

Keep in mind, sister. If everything is coming your way, you're in the wrong lane.

But if you look hard enough, you will always find some beauty in the ugliest of days. Sometimes, though, you have to search your own heart to find it. That might be the first place you find it. And that just might be the only place you find it for that day. But the good news? You found it.

And nothing, my friend, shines brighter than a kind heart.

And for Heaven's sake, take a chance or two. Nothing too crazy or off the wall, just live on the edge a little. Chances we take are part of growing into who we need to be. Kinda like when a toddler takes a chance and makes that first step. Chances can remind us of the beauty of imperfections in life. And to keep forging ahead. Just like that toddler learning to walk. The first thing that sweet baby does is get up and try it again. Forge ahead with another chance. And like that toddler, we'll eventually get it right.

Several years ago, I took a chance.

This chance came after many other chances. Chances that didn't give me butterflies. Chances that didn't make me blush. Chances that didn't make me feel like that was a chance I wanted to take any more.

By taking this new chance, I knew I was gambling on possible heartache. More disappointment and hurt. But I also knew I was gambling on possible happiness. Maybe a friendship and contentment.

Just as fear set in, something in my heart whispered, *"You'll either learn to fly or I will catch you. Just be bold."*

So bold I was.

I decided to do it. I jumped. I took the chance.

A chance that changed my life for the better. Actually, it changed it for the best.

By taking that chance, I found life was like a newfound garden. And growing in that garden I found beautiful flowers of love, joy, and peace. Patience, kindness, and generosity bloomed. Then, I found faithfulness, gentleness, and self-control flourishing.

However, of all the beauty found in this garden? The greatest was love.

It also grew ugly, smothering weeds of tears, uncertainties, and doubt. Anger, irritations, and frustrations did their best to find a place to thrive.

I had to decide which I was going to water and nurture in my so-called newfound garden. The beautiful flowers or the smothering weeds?

This chance I took led me to a new life. It has made me a better me. A stronger me. It has taught me lessons of compassion. Lessons of forgiveness. Lessons of compromise.

It has taught me how to be bold and to stand firm. As well as how to be cautious and when to take a step back. It taught me the meaning of that old southern saying, *"From the grit comes a pearl."*

When things don't go just as we expect, like maybe an unexpected change of our plans or an abrupt complication in life that we just can't for the life of Moses figure out why it happened? That's the grit in life. It hurts. It's irritating. It lies to us. It tells us we've gone as far as we're gonna go. It wants us to stop and just stay right where we are. Just give up. But as long as we keep fighting through, trusting His promises, and knowing we will come out of this race better and stronger than we started, we will start to see the beauty. We will shine. We will grow. We will get to that peace and joy in life that we all so much deserve. It is then we are becoming the pearl.

The chance I took?

Oh, right.

I took a chance on love. Something I had written off and planned to never allow to be a part of my future.

But the plans being made now were no longer mine.

It seems someone greater than me who prepared a path just for me had taken over. And, oh, how I wish He would have taken the lead years ago.

I fell in love.

Something I never expected. Something I never saw coming. Something I was never prepared for.

You see, he was cute.

Quite possibly the cutest boy in the world.

GALATIANS 5:22-23

But the fruit of the Spirit is love, joy, peace,
patience, kindness, goodness, faithfulness, gentleness,
self-control: against such things there is no law.

CPSIA information can be obtained
at www.ICGtesting.com
Printed in the USA
LVHW041724231020
669603LV00005B/82

9 781646 631995